Studying and living in Britain

The British Council's Guide

University Press of Mississippi/Jackson

First published 1949
Completely revised and rewritten 1996

Published in the United Kingdom by
Northcote House Publishers Ltd

First published in the United States of America in 1997 by
University Press of Mississippi

00 99 98 97 4 3 2 1

Library of Congress Cataloging-in-Publication Data
Studying and living in Britain: the British Council's guide/the
British Council.
    p. cm.
Originally published: Plymouth, U.K.: Northcote House, 1996.
Includes index.

ISBN 0-87805-987-3 (pbk.)

1. Foreign study – Great Britain – Guidebooks. 2. Education,
Higher – Great Britain – Guidebooks. 3. Great Britain – Guidebooks.
I. British Council.
LB2376.6.G7S782 1997
370. 116-dc21   96-40398 CIP

British Library Cataloguing-in-Publication Data available
Designed and produced by the British Council
DPX/C398
Printed in Great Britain by The Guernsey Press

Cartoons by Mike Flanagan; cover photograph
Telegraph Colour Library

The British Council is registered in England as a charity no. 209131

Contents

Foreword

As a prospective international student wishing to study in Britain you will find a great variety of educational opportunities, whether you are looking for general education or for vocational and professional training. You will find institutions ranging in size from under one thousand to forty thousand students, located in rural areas as well as major cities and towns. However, the fact that there is such a wide choice means that you will need to look very carefully at all your options to ensure that you choose the course of study that best suits your personal circumstances. Although some of you may be able to come to Britain in advance, as 'prospective students' to find out more about the course that interests you, most of you will have to gather all the information, and make important decisions before you arrive.

Although this book is not a comprehensive guide to the system of education and training in Britain, we aim to provide three types of information so you know:

- what kinds of opportunities exist;
- where to obtain the more detailed information;
- the practical implications of coming to Britain to study.

Every effort has been made to ensure that the information given in the book is correct at the time of going to print. However, please remember that, in some areas, the situation can change quite frequently. Wherever possible we advise you how to check on the latest situation.

1 Opportunities for study in Britain

1.1 Choosing a course

Although you probably already know which subject or subjects you wish to study, you will still have to consider which type of course will best suit your needs. There are still many different types of course to choose from – ranging from purely academic courses to those which will provide you with training for a specific job. The variety of educational opportunities in Britain is enormous, and before making any decisions you will need to ask yourself several questions. First: 'Why do I want to take the course?' It is likely that the reason you have decided to take a course is to gain a qualification, either because it is the entry requirement for another course you want to take, or because it is a qualification you need in order to be considered for a particular job or career. Therefore the second question you need to ask is: 'What qualification do I hope to obtain at the end of the course?' As an international student it is also very important to make sure that the qualification you hope to obtain will be recognized and accepted by employers in your home country, or by the college or university where you intend to continue your studies. Another consideration is the course content: 'Does the course cover everything I need?' There are courses which may have similar titles but which focus on different aspects of the subject. It is also important to think about the range of options available within the course: how much of the course will be compulsory and to what extent will you be able to design your own programme? Finally you need to ask yourself: 'Do I have the relevant qualifications to fulfil the entry requirements of the course?'

1.2 Which qualifications can be obtained in Britain?

In Britain you can study for a wide range of qualifications, particularly at the pre-degree level. Depending on the type of career you wish to follow, you may decide to take vocational or professional qualifications which equip and qualify you for a particular job, or academic qualifications which may not necessarily lead to a specific career but will provide you with a full knowledge of a subject and a basis for possible study at a higher level. In general, courses leading

'In Britain you can study for a wide range of qualifications'

to vocational qualifications emphasize the practical rather than the theoretical aspects of a particular subject.

Pre-degree level
Courses are offered by:

- schools;
- sixth-form colleges;
- colleges of further education;
- colleges of higher education;
- independent colleges;
- universities.

General Certificate of Secondary Education (GCSE)
In England and Wales, GCSE examinations replaced O level examinations some time ago. However, in some countries overseas, students are still able to take O levels and this qualification is still recognized by colleges and universities in Britain. Most students take GCSEs while they are at secondary school when they are aged around fifteen or sixteen. GCSEs can be taken in a wide range of subjects, and usually students take between five and ten subjects at

any one time. GCSE courses normally take two years and are assessed by coursework and written examination at the end of the course. For each examination passed you will be awarded a grade between A and G with A being the highest and G the lowest.

A levels and AS levels
A levels are still the most common way of fulfilling the entry requirements for degree courses. Most students in Britain start preparing for A-level examinations when they are aged around sixteen or seventeen and courses normally last for two years, although some independent colleges and some colleges of further education offer intensive one-year A-level courses. Students usually take between two and four subjects at one time and will normally be expected to have a GCSE or equivalent qualification in the subject they wish to take at A level. Assessment for most subjects is in the form of written examination at the end of the course. Passes are graded between A and E with A being the highest. An AS level is of an equivalent standard to an A level but has half the subject content. In terms of entrance requirements for a degree course, two AS levels count as one A level. AS levels are sometimes taken by students who feel that it is too early to specialize and wish to take a wider variety of subjects.

Scottish Certificate of Education (SCE)
The Scottish Certificate of Education S grade (Standard grade) is equivalent to GCSE while the H grade (Higher certificate) is roughly equivalent to A level. SCE Higher certificates prepare students for entry to Scottish universities, although A levels are also accepted.

Business and Technology Education Council (BTEC) qualifications
BTEC courses are available in over two hundred subjects and are often taken as an alternative to GCSEs and A levels. BTEC Certificates and Diplomas can be obtained at three different levels: BTEC First (equivalent to GCSE) which takes one year, BTEC National (equivalent to A and AS level) which takes two years and BTEC Higher National (HND) (comparable to two years of an undergraduate degree) which can take between two and three years. Many BTEC courses will include work-related projects or a period of work experience. BTEC awards are widely accepted by universities and many students transfer from HND courses on to the final year of a degree course.

Scottish Vocational Education Council (SCOTVEC) qualifications

In Scotland a similar range of vocational qualifications is available.

Other vocational qualifications

There are several other major examining boards awarding vocational qualifications in specific areas of study. Royal Society of Arts (RSA) qualifications are awarded in a variety of areas such as business studies, secretarial studies, foreign-language teaching, marketing, journalism and computer studies. The London Chamber of Commerce and Industry (LCCI) awards qualifications in commercial and managerial areas. The City and Guilds of London Institute (City and Guilds) offers a wide range of qualifications in many areas as diverse as engineering and catering.

General National Vocational Qualifications (GNVQs)

Because of the rather wide range of different academic and vocational qualifications available at pre-degree level and the many different examining boards in existence, the British government has introduced a national framework of vocational qualifications. The intention is not only to provide an alternative to GCSEs and A levels but also to narrow the divide between skills-based vocational education and the more traditional academic education, so that students may more easily transfer between the two different routes. College-based GNVQs exist at three levels: Foundation (level 1), Intermediate (level 2 – equivalent to GCSE) and Advanced (level 3 – equivalent to A level). Assessment is by coursework rather than written examination. Most of the current vocational examining boards (including BTEC, RSA, City and Guilds) can award GNVQs and it is likely that most other vocational qualifications will eventually be replaced by GNVQs.

Scottish Vocational Qualifications (SVQs)

The Scottish equivalent of GNVQs.

The International Baccalaureate (IB)

A two-year course involving the study of six different subjects, the International Baccalaureate is accepted by universities in Britain and throughout the world as an alternative to A levels.

Undergraduate and postgraduate degree level
Courses are offered by universities and by colleges of higher education.

Undergraduate degrees
Undergraduate degrees, or first degrees, normally take three years to complete in England and Wales and four years in Scotland. Degrees which include a period of work experience (sandwich courses) take longer. At some universities and colleges, students studying for degrees in certain subjects (for example art and design) are required to take a foundation course followed by a three-year degree course. Courses leading to degrees in medicine, dentistry and architecture can take up to seven years to complete. Degrees can be awarded for study of a single subject, a combination of two subjects (joint degree) or, on modular degree courses, three or more subjects. Depending on the subject or subjects being studied, successful students will be awarded one of the following: BA, B.Sc., B.Ed., B.Eng., LL.B. Degrees are graded and successful students may be awarded a first-class honours degree, an upper second-class honours degree (2i), a lower second-class honours degree (2ii) or a third-class honours degree. Students who do not achieve the standard required for an honours degree will be awarded an ordinary degree.

Postgraduate degrees
After completing a first degree, students can continue their studies by taking a postgraduate course. Postgraduate courses can lead to:

- postgraduate certificates and diplomas;
- master's degrees;
- research degrees.

Postgraduate certificates and diplomas normally take one year to complete. The courses are often vocational in nature and students holding these awards can sometimes gain exemption from some professional examinations (see section below on professional qualifications). Master's degrees are normally obtained by taught courses leading to an award such as MA, M.Sc., M.Eng., M.Tech., MBA or LL.M. Students obtaining a master's degree by research are normally awarded an M.Phil. Most taught master's courses last for one year. They will consist of lectures, seminars, training in research methods, practical work where relevant, coursework, and a written and sometimes spoken examination (called a viva). Some courses will also include a research project which has to be written up as a short thesis or dissertation. Master's degrees obtained by research can take up to two years. Master's degrees are not graded although some universities may award a distinction for outstanding performance. Some master's courses will provide exemption from professional examinations. A doctoral degree (Ph.D.) is awarded after completion of a thesis which sets out the results and conclusions of original research in a specific area. A doctorate can take three years or more to complete. Students are supervised but rarely attend formal lectures.

Professional qualifications

Courses are offered by:

- independent colleges;
- colleges of further education;
- colleges of higher education;
- universities.

In many professions, for example accountancy, architecture, banking and law, professional institutions exist to set and monitor standards in the profession and to encourage the exchange of ideas. Membership of a professional institution often depends on passing the institution's own examinations and in some cases it is obligatory to obtain membership of the relevant institution before you can practise in your chosen profession. Many colleges and some universities offer courses leading to various professional qualifications. Before applying, however, it is important to make sure that the qualification you will gain is recognized in your home country. If you already have a relevant degree or vocational qualification you may be given exemption from certain parts of the course.

There are some professions, such as nursing, medicine and dentistry, where there are very strict regulations covering courses and qualifications. Anyone wishing to train in these areas should make sure that they obtain detailed information from the relevant professional body. Information on postgraduate medical opportunities for overseas doctors is available from the British Council's National Advice Centre for Postgraduate Medical Education (address at the end of this chapter).

Routes through the British education system

Students in Britain who have a clear view of what they want to do
once they have finished their education often follow one of the routes
illustrated in the diagram below.

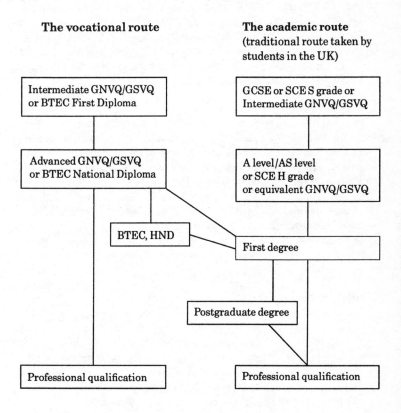

The vocational route

The academic route
(traditional route taken by
students in the UK)

| Intermediate GNVQ/GSVQ or BTEC First Diploma | GCSE or SCE S grade or Intermediate GNVQ/GSVQ |

| Advanced GNVQ/GSVQ or BTEC National Diploma | A level/AS level or SCE H grade or equivalent GNVQ/GSVQ |

BTEC, HND

First degree

Postgraduate degree

Professional qualification

Professional qualification

As an international student from overseas, you will probably be
coming to Britain with some qualifications you have already
obtained in your home country. Provided that you fulfil the entry
requirements specified by the college or university to which you are
applying you may enter at any point along any of the routes.

1.3   Entry requirements

Once you have chosen which course you wish to study, it is important to make sure that you have the appropriate entry requirements. As you can see from the diagram on the previous page, the traditional GCSE and A-level route is no longer the only way of getting on to a British degree course. Entry requirements will vary from one institution to another, and holding the minimum qualifications for entry does not guarantee a place on a course as there are often more applicants than places available.

Overseas qualifications

Although entry requirements are normally stated in terms of British qualifications, you may find that the qualifications you have gained in your home country are accepted by colleges and universities in Britain. You can check how your own qualifications compare to British qualifications by contacting your local British Council office or by writing to the National Academic Recognition Information Centre (see address list at the end of this chapter). You should be aware, however, that it is up to each individual college and university to decide which, if any, overseas qualifications it will accept, so you must also check this with the institution before making your application.

Advanced standing

If you have reached a certain level of education in your home country, it may be possible to be admitted directly on to the second, or even third, year of a degree course at a British college or university. If you think that you might be eligible to do this, you should contact the university or college directly, telling them what qualifications you already have and asking whether you may be exempt from any part of the course you wish to take.

Access, bridging and foundation courses

If your own school-leaving qualifications do not quite match UK university entry requirements, you may be advised to take an access or bridging course. Typically lasting for six months to one year, these courses prepare students for degree-level work. Quite often, they are linked to a particular area of study, for example an access course for students who wish to study engineering. However most will include help with English language for academic purposes and study skills.

Some also provide training in information technology and basic mathematics. The courses are usually run by colleges of further or higher education, although many are linked to a particular university so that students successfully completing the access course will be guaranteed a place at that university. A number of British colleges and universities now have links with institutions overseas and you may find a college in your home country running an access course which prepares students for study at a particular college or university in Britain. Details of these should be available from your local British Council office.

Other routes to British higher education

Many colleges and universities overseas now have formal agreements with partner institutions in Britain allowing their own students to take part of their course at a college or university in Britain. This means, for example, that you may start a course at your home college or university and then in your second or final year come to Britain to complete your qualification at the partner institution. Again, your local British Council office should have information about institutions which have formal links with British colleges and universities.

1.4   English language requirements

In order to gain maximum benefit from your stay in Britain, it is essential that you have a good command of the English language. Most colleges and universities in Britain will ask you to have reached a certain level of competency in English before admitting you on to a course. It is likely that you will be asked for evidence that you have obtained a certain grade or score in a recognized test or examination. Different institutions, and even different courses, will have different requirements and it is important to check this with the college or university to which you are applying, but normally any one of the following will be accepted:

- the British Council International English Language Testing Service (IELTS) test (minimum score 6). This test can be taken in 180 centres in 110 countries and the results are recognized by all colleges and universities in Britain;
- the Cambridge (UCLES) Certificate of Proficiency in English (grade C or above);

- the Cambridge (UCLES) Certificate of Advanced English (grade C or above);
- English language O level or GCSE;
- NEAB test in English for overseas students (grade three or above) and the NEAB test in English for speakers of other languages (Pass);
- the Test of English as a Foreign Language (TOEFL) (score 550). This is an American test.

ⓘ Your local British Council office should be able to tell you when and where any of these tests can be taken.

Language support at colleges and universities
Most colleges and universities in Britain provide some form of English language support for their own students. Some run pre-sessional language courses, normally in the summer prior to the start of the first term. The institution to which you have applied may advise you to attend a pre-sessional English course, or even make attendance a condition of your acceptance on to a course. Others may test your English on arrival and recommend that you take in-sessional language classes alongside your academic study. Sometimes these classes will be provided free of charge.

Learning English in Britain
You may of course, wish to come to Britain just to study English language, either to gain a qualification or simply for pleasure. There are hundreds of public (state) and private schools and colleges offering courses in English language at all levels. You will find a huge variety of different types of course: courses lasting from one week to one year, courses which combine the study of English with a holiday or recreational activity, courses which teach English for a specific purpose (for example, English for business, English for doctors). You may be learning English in order to gain a qualification which will allow you to teach English back home. In this case you will need to take a recognized TEFL qualification such as those offered by the RSA/Cambridge or Trinity College London examination boards. Because there is such a wide variety of colleges and courses, it is important to choose carefully because standards also vary. Your local British Council office will be a good source of information on English language courses in Britain. Three further sources of information are: the British Association of State Colleges

in English Language Teaching (BASCELT) which publishes a handbook providing details of courses offered at state colleges in Britain, the Association of Recognized English Language Services (ARELS) which provides a list of privately run English language schools which have been recognized by the British Council, and FIRST, who provide further information of privately run language schools which are also recognized by the British Council. Addresses for these organizations can be found in section 1.8.

1.5   Choosing a college or university

Once you have decided which course you want to study, the next thing to decide is where to study. There are several key questions you need to ask yourself. First: 'Which type of institution offers the course I want to take?' The answer to this question will depend on the type of course you are taking. For example, a postgraduate course will only be available at a university. Second: 'Which institution offers the course which best suits my requirements?' Here, you will be considering things like course content, teaching and examination methods, course length and cost of courses offered. Third: 'Where in Britain do I want to live?' You will be spending perhaps three or four years of your life here, so it is important to make the right decision. Fourth: 'Which institution offers all the facilities I would like to have?' For example, if you are keen on a certain type of sport it will be important for you to find an institution which offers facilities for that sport. Accommodation facilities are also a very important consideration. Finally, if you are considering postgraduate study, particularly a research degree, it is important to check out the specific department you will be in and, if possible, find out who your supervisor will be.

Different types of institution
Post-school education institutions in Britain come under a variety of different names and titles but they can be broadly divided into the categories below. Colleges of further education (FE) offer a wide range of courses from GCSE to, on occasions, degree level. Other institutions which offer courses at the FE level are: sixth-form colleges, technical colleges, community colleges, colleges of art and technology and other specialist colleges such as the College of Printing and the College of Food and Fashion. Colleges of higher education (HE) normally offer courses leading to degrees, post-

UK universities

Robert Gordon
Aberdeen

Middlesex University
Brunel University
University of North London
Thames Valley University
University of Westminster
City University
University of East London
London Guildhall University
University of London
South Bank University
University of Greenwich
Kingston University

Dundee
Abertay, Dundee
St Andrews
Stirling
Glasgow Caledonian
Strathclyde
Glasgow
Paisley
Napier
Edinburgh
Heriot-Watt

Northumbria at Newcastle
Newcastle
Sunderland
Durham
Teesside

Ulster (Coleraine)

Belfast

Lancaster
York
Hull
Central Lancashire
Bradford
Humberside
Leeds
Leeds Metropolitan
UMIST
Huddersfield
Liverpool
Manchester
Salford
Sheffield
Sheffield Hallam
Bangor
Liverpool John Moores
Manchester Metropolitan
Staffordshire
Nottingham
Keele
Nottingham Trent
Derby
Wolverhampton
Loughborough
Leicester
Aberystwyth
Birmingham
Aston
Central England in Birmingham
Warwick
Coventry
De Montfort
East Anglia
Lampeter
Cambridge
Open University
Buckingham
Cranfield
Essex
Glamorgan
Luton
Hertfordshire
Swansea
UWCM
Oxford
Anglia PU
Cardiff
Oxford Brookes
London
Bristol
Reading
Bath
Kent
University of the West of England
Surrey
Southampton
Sussex
Brighton
Exeter
Portsmouth
Bournemouth
Plymouth

graduate qualifications, professional and vocational qualifications. These can include: colleges of education, colleges of art and design, agricultural colleges, schools of music, schools of drama, business schools and medical schools. Universities are also colleges of higher education.

Private or independent colleges are those schools and colleges which are independent of government control. They offer courses ranging from GCSEs to, occasionally, degree-level studies. Although independent schools and colleges are not monitored by the government as state colleges are, if they are offering nationally recognized qualifications such as BTEC or RSA certificates and diplomas, they must be approved by those organizations. There is another organization called The British Accreditation Council for Independent Further and Higher Education (BAC) which also inspects and approves private colleges. As this accreditation is voluntary on the part of the colleges who choose to apply for accreditation from BAC, it cannot be assumed that any college not accredited is an inferior college. The British Council recommends however that, wherever possible, students opting for private-sector education choose an accredited college, as it has been independently assessed and approved.

Although accrediting bodies check the facilities at private colleges, they do not validate the qualifications offered. Students should therefore check that qualifications will be suitable for their purposes.

Content, length and cost of courses

Although two different institutions might offer what sounds like the same course, for example BA English Literature, the actual content of the course may be quite different. One course may focus on Shakespeare or Chaucer while another may not offer Shakespeare at all but concentrate on modern literature instead. It is up to you to find out if a particular course covers all the topics you require. Make sure that you know how long the course will take to complete and that you will be able to afford the fees and living expenses for the whole course. If one institution is offering you the same course but for less time than another institution, make sure that all the areas you need are covered. This is particularly important if you are taking a course leading to an examination set by an external examining board. Different institutions may also charge different fees. It is also important to check what the quoted fee does and does not cover. For example, will there be an extra charge for use of laboratories or studios? Will you need to pay for essential materials in an art or design course? Will you have to pay extra for field trips?

Teaching and examination methods

Teaching methods used in universities and colleges of higher education may differ from those used in schools and some other colleges. In general, in higher education you are encouraged to take much more responsibility for your own learning rather than attend classes all the time. Different institutions may place the emphasis on different learning styles: formal lectures, small discussion groups (seminars), private study, project and practical work, or a combination of some or all of these. As the use of different teaching methods can affect your studies, you should give some thought to which of these suit you best. Assessment methods can also differ from course to course. Few institutions base their assessment of a student totally on end-of-year examination. It is more likely that you will be assessed on a combination of written coursework, project work, performance in seminars and examinations.

Location

Although Britain is relatively small, there is a wide variety of landscapes and environments. The flat fens and coastline of East Anglia, for example, contrast sharply to the lakes and mountains of Scotland and the far north of England. The bustle of a big city like London or Manchester may be your choice but others might prefer smaller and quieter country towns. Only you can decide which environment will suit you best. You may also have to choose between a campus or a non-campus institution. A campus institution is one where all the facilities, including classrooms, accommodation, library and sports facilities, are concentrated all together on one site, either in one area of a city centre or just outside the suburbs. This means that everything is easily accessible and, if you wish, you can immerse yourself in student life twenty-four hours a day. Non-campus institutions have their facilities spread over a wider area. This means that you may have to travel across town for lectures or to use the library but it will also provide you with the opportunity to gain a wider experience of day-to-day life in Britain.

Facilities

Only you know what facilities you would like a college or university to provide. Some of the things you might want to consider before making your choice might be:

- Does the institution have its own accommodation, for example, halls of residence?
- Does it guarantee a place in a hall of residence to students from overseas?
- If not, is there an accommodation office to help students find private accommodation?
- Does the institution have its own library?
- Does it have its own sports facilities, or are there nearby facilities which can be used by students?
- Is there a refectory which caters for special dietary requirements?
- Does the institution have facilities which will allow you to practise your own religion?
- Is there a student welfare service?
- Does the institution provide an orientation course for new students? Is it free of charge?
- Are there facilities for students with disabilities?

1.6　How to apply

Different types of institutions and different courses have different application procedures. Details of how and when to apply for a course will be given in the prospectus. Methods of application can be divided into two main types: applications made through a central admissions system and applications made directly to the institution.

Applications made through a central admissions system
- All undergraduate degree-level courses and HND courses at universities except the University of Buckingham and the Open University (UCAS/ADAR).
- Degree-level courses and HND courses at some colleges of higher education (UCAS).
- Non-degree level courses in nursing (NMCCH).
- Postgraduate Certificate of Education (teacher training) (GTTR).
- Postgraduate courses in art and design (ADAR).
- Most qualifications in social work, undergraduate and postgraduate (SWAS).

Each system will have its own application form, application guidelines and application deadline. Details should be obtained by writing directly to the relevant body (addresses are given at the end of this chapter).

UCAS (Universities and Colleges Admissions System)
All courses included in the UCAS scheme are listed in the UCAS handbook which should be available for reference in local British Council offices or can be obtained (free of charge) by writing directly to UCAS. Using one application form, you may apply for up to six degree or HND courses. The current application fee is £12 and should be sent to UCAS with the completed application form. The deadline for receipt of applications is 15 December prior to the year you wish to start your course (or 15 October if you are applying to the Universities of Oxford and Cambridge). You can apply after this date but many courses may already be full by then. Each institution to which you have applied will consider your application and respond to you via UCAS. Follow the diagram on next page to see what happens next.

ADAR (Art and Design Admissions Registry)
This is the admissions system used if you are applying for most art and design courses other than undergraduate courses at a university. The process is similar to the UCAS system except that, through ADAR, you can only choose up to four courses to apply for. The deadline for applications is 31 March prior to the start of the course. In order to cover administration costs there is a fee of £16 (if you are from a country in the European Union) or £30 (for those living elsewhere). This fee should be sent to ADAR when requesting an application form.

NMCCH (Nurses and Midwives Central Clearing House)
With the exception of degree-level courses at universities, all applications for nursing courses in England should go through the NMCCH. There is a fee of £6 which should be sent when requesting an application form. The deadline for receipt of completed forms is 13 December. Applications for courses in Scotland should be made through the Centralised Application to Nurse Training Clearing House (CATCH). Applications for courses in Wales and Northern Ireland should be made directly to the institution concerned.

UCAS application procedures

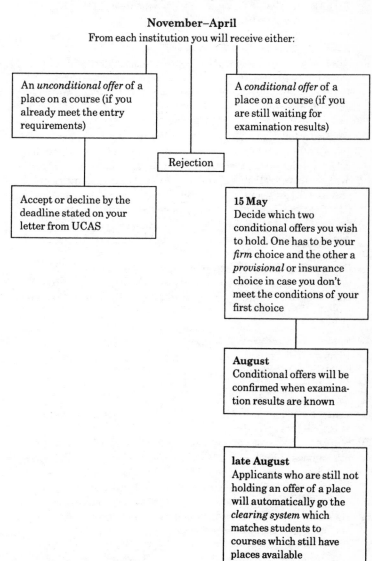

November–April
From each institution you will receive either:

An *unconditional offer* of a place on a course (if you already meet the entry requirements)

A *conditional offer* of a place on a course (if you are still waiting for examination results)

Rejection

Accept or decline by the deadline stated on your letter from UCAS

15 May
Decide which two conditional offers you wish to hold. One has to be your *firm* choice and the other a *provisional* or insurance choice in case you don't meet the conditions of your first choice

August
Conditional offers will be confirmed when examination results are known

late August
Applicants who are still not holding an offer of a place will automatically go the *clearing system* which matches students to courses which still have places available

GTTR (Graduate Teacher Training Registry)
All applications for Postgraduate Certificate of Education (PGCE) courses should be made through the GTTR.

SWAS (Social Work Admissions System)
For courses leading to the Diploma in Social Work, you should apply through SWAS. Further information can be obtained from the Central Council for Education and Training in Social Work (address at the end of this chapter).

Applications made directly to the institution
For all other courses, applications must be made directly to the school, college or university concerned. When you are applying directly to an institution, you may apply for as many different places you like. To give your application the best chance, apply as early as possible. The demand for places on courses usually exceeds the number of places available and institutions start processing applications up to eighteen months before the start of the course.

Completing the application form
Whether you are applying directly to an institution or through a central system, there are a few guidelines you should follow when completing the form.

✅ Make sure there are no spelling mistakes or alterations. It is advisable to photocopy the form before filling it in so that you can practise on the photocopied version.

✅ Also keep a copy of the final version for your own reference.

✅ Use black ink and write in block capitals. These forms will be photocopied many times by institutions and it is important that your writing remains legible.

✅ Where the form asks for surname or family name decide which of your names you are going to use here and remember which you have used. This will be the name which will appear on all correspondence and databases. If you need to contact the institution later on, don't give another name as they won't be able to find your application.

✅ Make full use of the section which asks you to provide further information about yourself and why you chose this particular course. This is your opportunity to 'sell yourself' as the institution really does want to know about you and your interests. Don't just say 'I like sport' or 'I like reading': say which sports or what sort of books you enjoy, and why. Explain why you have chosen the course for which you are applying and briefly mention your long-term aims.

1.7   Checklists

Before finally choosing a course, ask yourself the following questions:

- ✅ Have I got the qualifications I need to take this course?
- ✅ If not, where can I obtain these qualifications?
- ✅ Will my current qualifications give me any exemptions from any part of this course?
- ✅ Which qualification will I obtain at the end of this course?
- ✅ Will this qualification by recognized by employers/institutions in my home country?

Before you decide which college or university to apply to, make sure that you have considered the following:

- ✅ What type of institution will best suit my needs?
- ✅ Which teaching and examination methods will be used and which suit me best?
- ✅ Have I seen an outline of the content of the course? Do I know exactly what I am going to be taught?
- ✅ Do I prefer a city or a rural environment? Would I prefer a large or small college, a modern or traditional one?
- ✅ Does the institution provide all the facilities I would like it to have?
- ✅ Can I afford the course fees?
- ✅ What other expenses will be involved and can I afford these too?
- ✅ Does the institution offer any scholarships?

1.8   Sources of information

Being an international student, it is unlikely that you will have the opportunity to visit a wide range of colleges and universities in Britain, therefore the most valuable source of information about an institution is its prospectus. The prospectus should contain information about course content, entry requirements, teaching and examination methods, facilities, location, and so on. All British Council offices should have a wide range of prospectuses for reference but if you write directly to the institution concerned they will send you a free copy. A good prospectus will provide answers to all the questions you will want to ask about an institution. If you cannot find the information you require in the prospectus, write to or telephone the institution directly to get the information you need.

In your own country, your local British Council office (or the British Embassy or High Commission) will also be able to provide information and advice. Information Provision Unit, Information Group, The British Council (Medlock Street, Manchester, M15 4AA, UK) publishes comprehensive information sheets about studying in the UK which are available from your local British Council office. These and other main sources of information are given below.

Addresses of organizations mentioned in this chapter

Art and Design Admissions Registry (ADAR), Penn House, 9 Broad Street, Hereford HR4 9AP, Tel: (0)1432 266653, Fax: (0)1432 343367.

Association of Recognized English Language Services (ARELS), 2 Pontypool Place, Valentines Place, London SE1 8QF, Tel: (0)171-242 3136, Fax: (0)171-928 9378.

British Accreditation Council for Independent Further and Higher Education (BAC), Suite 401, 27 Marylebone Road, London NW1 5JS, Tel: (0)171-487 4643, Fax: (0)171-486 4253.

British Association of State Colleges in English Language Teaching (BASCELT), The Lodge, Francis Close Hall, Swindon Road, Cheltenham, Gloucestershire GL50 4AZ, Tel: (0)1242 227099, Fax: (0)1242 227055.

Business and Technology Education Council (BTEC), Central House, Upper Woburn Place, London WC1H 0HH, Tel: (0)171-413 8400, Fax: (0)171-387 6068.

Centralised Application to Nurse Training Clearing House (CATCH), PO Box 21, Edinburgh EH2 1NT, Tel: (0)131-226 7999, Fax: (0)131-226 2942.

Central Council for Education and Training in Social Work (CCETSW), Derbyshire House, St Chad's Street, London WC1H 8AD, Tel: (0)171-278 2455.

City and Guilds of London Institute, 1 Giltspur Street, London EC1A 9DD, Tel: (0)171-294 2468.

FIRST, 4 Russetts Drive (F), Fleet, Hampshire GU13 9QE, Tel: (0)1252 815524, Fax: (0)1252 815525. Web address: http://www.edunet.com/first.

The Graduate Teacher Training Registry (GTTR), Fulton House, Jessop Avenue, Cheltenham, Gloucestershire GL50 3SH, Tel: (0)1242 225868,Fax: (0)1242 26355.

The London Chamber of Commerce and Industry (LCCI), 33 Queen Street, London EC4R 1AP, Tel: (0)171-248 4444, Fax: (0)171-489 0391.

The National Academic Recognition Information Centre (NARIC), The British Council, Medlock Street, Manchester M5 4AA, Tel: (0)161-957 7065, Fax: (0)161-957 7561.

The National Advice Centre for Postgraduate Medical Education (NACPME), Third Floor, The British Council, Medlock Street, Manchester M15 4AA, Tel: (0)161-957 7218, Fax: (0)161-957 7724.

The National Council for Vocational Qualifications (NCVQ), 222 Euston Road, London NW1 2BZ, Tel: (0)171-387 9898, Fax: (0)171-387 0978.

The Nurses and Midwives Central Clearing House (NMCCH), PO Box 9017, London W1A 0XA, Tel: (0)171-391 6305.

The Royal Society of Arts (RSA) Examinations Board, Westwood Way, Coventry CV4 8HS, Tel: (0)1203 470033, Fax: (0)1203 468080.

The Scottish Vocational Education Council (SCOTVEC), 24 Douglas House, Glasgow G2 7NG, Tel: (0)141-248 7900, Fax: (0)141-242 2244.

Trinity College London, 16 Park Crescent, London W1N 4AP, Tel: (0) 171-323 2328, Fax: (0)171-323 5201.

The University of Cambridge Local Examinations Syndicate (UCLES), 1 Hills Road, Cambridge CB1 2EU, Tel: (0)1223 553311, Fax: (0)1223 460278.

The Universities and Colleges Admissions Service (UCAS), Fulton House, Jessop Avenue, Cheltenham, Gloucestershire GL50 3SH, Tel: (0)1242 222444, Fax: (0)1242 221622.

Further reading
You may find the following publications useful. Many of them will be available for reference at most British Council offices overseas, or at your own school or college library or careers office.

British Council information sheets: *Application procedures; Postgraduate study; Private colleges accreditation; Sources of financial assistance for overseas students; Taking a first degree; Tuition fees and the cost of living.*

British Qualifications, Kogan Page, annual.

British Universities Guide to Graduate Study, CVCP, annual.

The Commonwealth Universities Yearbook, ACU, annual.

Degree Course Guides, CRAC, Hobsons Publishing Plc, annual.

Directory of Further Education, CRAC, Hobsons Publishing Plc, annual.

Directory of Higher Education, CRAC, Hobsons Publishing Plc, annual.

Directory of Technical and Further Education, Pitman, 1995, £75.00.

Entrance Guide to Higher Education in Scotland, John Smith and Jones, 1996, £6.00.

Graduate Studies, CRAC, Hobsons Publishing Plc, annual.

Higgins, Tony *How to complete your UCAS application form for 1996 entry*, Trotman, 1995, £5.95.

Higher Education in the UK, Longman, annual.
NARIC, *International Guide to Qualifications in Education*, Mansell Publishing Ltd, 1996, £100.00.

The Student Book: the applicant's indispensable guide to UK colleges and universities, Macmillan, 1996, £12.99.
UKCOSA sheets: *Choosing the right course and college; Financial help and course fees and grants; Scholarships for international students* (available from your local British Council office).

University Entrance: the Official Guide, Sheed and Ward, annual.

Where to Study in the UK: A Guide to British Professional Qualifications, Kogan Page, 1988, £8.95.

Which Degree in Britain, CRAC, Hobsons Publishing Plc, annual.

2 Before you leave home – preparing to come to Britain

Once you have decided to study in Britain, and have been accepted on to a course, there are many practical arrangements to be made. Some of these arrangements need to be made well in advance.

2.1 Passports and immigration

Before you make any other arrangements to travel, you must make sure that you have all the documentation required to enter the United Kingdom (UK) and to stay for the duration of your course. In order to enter the UK everyone, except for students from countries belonging to the European Union (EU) or the European Economic Area (EEA), must produce a valid international passport. Many of you will also be required to obtain some form of entry clearance. For details of the UK immigration regulations, please refer to Chapter 3 of this book.

'You must ... have all the documents required to enter the UK'

2.2 Accommodation

Once you have accepted an offer of a place on a course, the institution should send you a package of information which should contain, amongst other things, details about the types of accommodation which will be available to you and how you should apply for it. If you do not receive this information, contact the institution urgently and ask when you can expect to receive it. It is very important that you know well in advance whether the institution will:

- provide you with accommodation either on or off campus;
- help you to find your own accommodation (some institutions may do this only once you have already arrived there); or
- provide no help with accommodation at all, leaving you responsible for finding you own place to live.

Whichever service the college or university provides, it is likely that there will be some kind of application form to complete. In order to secure your accommodation or take advantage of any services offered, it is important that you return this form by the deadline given. If you are being offered a place in university or college-owned accommodation, for example, a hall of residence, it is advisable that you take it. Private accommodation is not easy to find, especially in September, when hundreds of other new students are also looking around for somewhere to live. Staying in a hall of residence may not be everyone's choice but at least it can provide you with a secure base from which you can get to know the surrounding area and decide where you might like to live after your first year in Britain. Further information about accommodation in Britain can be found in Chapter 5 of this book.

Arranging temporary accommodation

If you have decided against university or college accommodation, or if your place of study does not provide it at all, you must arrange for somewhere to stay temporarily while you are looking for your permanent accommodation. You should not plan to arrive in Britain without knowing where you are going to stay, at least for the first few nights. There are several options open to you.

Some universities and colleges rent out rooms in their halls of residence on a temporary basis several weeks before the start of the term. This is usually the cheapest option and the accommodation may be conveniently located near to your place of study. However, the disadvantage is that you will have to move out by a specified time.

Student hostels, which are privately run and not attached to any particular college or university, sometimes provide accommodation for short stays. A list of student hostels can be found in Appendix 2.

ⓘ Hostels and guest houses are expensive options for long-term accommodation but may be your preferred choice for short-term accommodation. Lists of hostels, guest houses and bed and breakfast accommodation can be obtained from the British Tourist Authority. If you write to them for information, don't forget to tell them which town or city you will be staying in.

2.3   Money

Before you come to Britain, you should make sure that you have enough money to cover your tuition fees and your living expenses for the duration of your course. It is important that you make adequate financial provision before you leave home as it may be difficult to obtain extra funds once you are in Britain. To avoid financial ⓔ problems, refer to Chapter 6 to find out how much money you will need.

Scholarships
If you wish to find out whether you are eligible for any scholarships, it is important to start making enquiries and applications well in advance – over a year in some cases. You can obtain information about available scholarships from your local British Council office or from the Ministry or Department of Education in your home country. Some colleges and universities in Britain also offer scholarships to students from overseas. Even if they have not sent details to you, it is worth enquiring to see whether the institution to which you have applied has any scholarships available. If you are unable to afford to come to Britain to study without a scholarship, it is vital that you obtain one before you leave home as it is unlikely that you will be able to arrange financial support once you have begun your studies. Further details about scholarships can be found in Chapter 6.

Foreign exchange
Although there is no limit to the amount of money you can bring into Britain, you need to check whether your own government has

restrictions on the amount of money you may take out of the country. If your country does have foreign exchange controls you will need to find out:

- how to obtain permission to transfer money and what documents are required;
- whether there is a limit to the amount that can be transferred;
- what are the regulations concerning foreign exchange and start making arrangements as soon as possible.

Currency transfer

It is advisable not to carry large sums of money with you when you travel. The best way of sending money overseas is by currency transfer. The following methods might be considered but your local bank should be able to provide you with full details:

- International money order – this can be paid into a bank account or, at some banks, used to obtain cash as long as you have your passport for identification. The value of an international money order will vary according to the exchange rate on the day it is used. A commission charge will also be deducted.
- Bank draft – this is similar to an international money order except that it must be paid into a bank account. If you are bringing a draft with you, or having one sent to you, you should make sure that it is made out to you in sterling (British currency) and drawn on a British bank. If the draft is in sterling then you will not be charged a commission and it will take less time to clear than if it is in your own currency.
- Telegraphic transfer – this is the quickest but most expensive way of having money sent overseas. However, money can only be transferred in this way once you have a bank account in Britain.

Money for your first few weeks in Britain

Depending on which method you use to transfer money, and how soon you are able to open a bank account (see Chapter 6), it could be anything between ten days and six weeks before you have access to your money. This means that you will need to bring a certain amount with you.

- *Sterling* – British currency (sterling) consists of pounds (£) and pence (p). One pound (£1) is divided into 100 pence (100p). Notes are issued for £50, £20, £10, £5 and coins for £1, 50p, 20p, 10p, 5p, 2p and 1p. You will need to bring a certain amount of cash for use on your journey and for when you first arrive at your destination. About £150 should be enough, although you may need more if you have a long journey between your point of arrival and your final destination.

- *Other currencies* – if you do not have any British currency, you can exchange foreign money or travellers' cheques at the seaport or airport of arrival in the UK where there will be a twenty-four-hour bank or *bureau de change*. If you are arriving in Britain at a time when banks are normally closed, it is vital not to leave the seaport or airport before you have obtained some British currency. Most banks in Britain are open between 9.30 a.m. and 4.30 p.m. from Monday to Friday.
- *Bureaux de change* are open for longer hours than banks but can normally only be found in town centres.
- *Travellers' cheques* – apart from money for your immediate requirements, you will need to have some money available to use while you are waiting for your banker's draft or transferred money to clear. Rather than carrying huge amounts of cash around with you it is safer to buy travellers' cheques, which are insured against loss or theft.
- *Credit cards* – most credit cards can be used in Britain, either to pay for purchases or to obtain money from cash machines outside banks. However, you should check with your own bank to find out how much you will be charged each time you use your card overseas.

2.4   Insurance

At the same time as you book your ticket to travel to Britain, you should enquire about travel insurance to cover yourself and your luggage on your journey. While you are packing, make a list of what you packed in each suitcase in case of loss, when you will need to make a claim. If you are bringing valuable items with you, for example, jewellery, musical instruments, camera equipment, CD player, and if these items are covered by an insurance policy back home, you should check the terms of this policy to see if they will be insured while they are out of the country. If they are not covered, you will need to take out a personal belongings insurance policy once you have arrived in Britain (see Chapter 6). If you are not covered by the British National Health Service (see Chapter 7), you will also need to arrange some form of health insurance for your stay in Britain.

2.5   What to bring with you

What to bring with you to Britain is very much a matter of personal need and preference. If you are coming by plane, it is important to check your baggage allowance as paying for excess baggage can be expensive. Most airlines allow 15–20kg. If you are arriving by sea, you are allowed to bring much more – but don't forget you will still have to carry it.

Clothing
The climate in Britain is variable and can be unpredictable. Temperatures average between 5° centigrade in the winter and 20° centigrade in the summer. If you are coming from a hot climate, you will need to obtain some clothing for cold weather. It may be easier and cheaper to buy this once you are in Britain but if you are arriving in September or October, it would be advisable to have at least a coat, sweater and an umbrella with you. In general, British students dress quite informally with the emphasis on comfort. However, you should bring at least one set of smart clothes with you for any formal occasions you may need to attend.

Electrical equipment
Before you pack any electrical equipment you should make sure that it is compatible with UK standards. The electricity supply in Britain works on 240 volts and 50 cycles (50Hz). Most plug sockets take three-pin (square-pin) plugs which can be bought in Britain and easily fitted on to your appliances. Otherwise you can use an adaptor. You will also probably have to change the fuse in the plug. The majority of plugs sold will be already fitted with a thirteen-amp fuse. This type of fuse is not suitable for many items such as stereo equipment, hairdryers and clocks, and so you will have to change it to a five- or three-amp fuse. The box or instruction leaflet which came with the item should tell you which fuse you need. Most electrical equipment that you will need can be bought in Britain but you will probably find that it is more expensive than in your home country.

Books

Books are problematic because they can be heavy but are also necessary items for students. You may find that many of the books you require will be cheaper in Britain. In any case, never rush out to buy all the books which appear on the reading lists sent to you by your college or university. You may only need to refer to some of these books once or twice and they will certainly be available in the library. You will also be able to buy second-hand books from former students. One essential book to bring with you, however, is a bi-lingual dictionary.

Other items

There are certain items which you are not allowed to bring into the UK. These include some foods, plants and wildlife, drugs and weapons. For further details about what can and cannot be brought into the UK, contact the British Embassy, High Commission or Consulate in your home country. If you are planning to bring items such as computer or hi-fi equipment, it is advisable also to bring with you the receipt showing when and where the equipment was bought. You may be asked to certify that this equipment is for your own use and not being permanently imported.

2.6   Checklists

There are many things you will need to do before you leave home. Use this checklist to make sure that you don't forget anything.

✅ Make sure you have received a letter of unconditional acceptance from the school, college or university.

✅ Make sure that you have enough money to cover your tuition fees and living expenses for the whole time you will be in Britain.

✅ Arrange for the transfer of money to Britain.

✅ Make sure you have a valid passport.

✅ Make sure you have fully understood the UK immigration regulations and obtained the relevant entry clearance from the British Embassy, High Commission or Consulate.

✅ Complete and return all forms required by your college or university – including accommodation forms.

✅ Arrange temporary accommodation if necessary.

✅ Buy tickets and travel insurance.

✅ Order British currency and traveller's cheques.

✅ Check your baggage allowance.

✅ Find out whether you will be covered by the British National Health Service while you are in Britain, and if not, take out a medical insurance policy.

✅ Check whether you need a medical certificate to enter Britain.

✅ If you are currently taking any prescribed drugs or medicines, obtain a letter of explanation from your doctor.

✅ Obtain at least three passport-sized photographs of yourself.

✅ Make sure you know exactly when and where you are supposed to arrive at your place of study.

✅ Plan your journey from your point of entry into Britain to your final destination.

✅ Ask your college or university to provide you with the telephone number of someone you can contact in case you have any problems on your journey.

✅ Label all your luggage with your name and address in Britain.

You will need the following documents on your journey (so don't pack them in your luggage!):

✅ letter of unconditional acceptance from your place of study;

✅ documentary evidence that you have enough money to pay your fees and support yourself while studying (e.g. recent bank statements, proof of scholarship, sponsor's letter);

✅ travel tickets;

✅ passport containing entry clearance where necessary;

✅ address and telephone number of your final destination;

✅ insurance documents;

✅ medical certificate (if required).

2.7   Sources of information

Address of the organization mentioned in this chapter
The British Tourist Authority, Thames Tower, Blacks Road, London W6 9EL, Tel: (0)181-846 9000, Fax: (0)181-563 0302.

Further reading
UKCOSA sheets: *Accommodation; Arriving in the UK; Travel arrangements (before arrival in the UK)* (available from your local British Council office).

3 Immigration requirements

In this chapter arrangements you should make for your entry into Britain are reviewed in more detail.

3.1 Entry requirements

It is very important for anyone entering Britain to comply with the UK immigration rules. For example, if you wish to study in Britain, then you need to ensure that you enter the country with permission to study or as a prospective student. You should not try to enter as a visitor and then try to change your status. The information below describes the immigration requirements for students at the time of writing. It is important to check with your local British Embassy, High Commission or Consulate that this information is still up to date as the immigration rules do change from time to time.

Apart from students from the European Union (EU) or the European Economic Area (EEA), all international students should obtain some form of entry clearance. There are two different types of entry clearance:

- visa – which is compulsory;
- entry certificate – which is optional but recommended.

The paragraphs below tell you which type of entry clearance you will need.

Visa nationals

Entry clearance for visa nationals is compulsory. This takes the form of a visa and you can obtain it from a British Embassy or High Commission or Consulate.

Anyone who is a citizen of one of the countries listed below must have a visa stamped in their passport before travelling to Britain: Afghanistan, Albania, Algeria, Angola, Armenia, Azerbaijan, Bangladesh, Belarus, Benin, Bhutan, Bosnia-Herzegovina, Bulgaria, Burkina Faso, Burma, Burundi, Cambodia, Cameroon, Cape Verde, Central African Republic, Chad, China, Comoros, Congo, Cuba,

Djibouti, Egypt, Equatorial Guinea, Eritrea, Ethiopia, Gabon, Georgia, Ghana, Guinea, Guinea-Bissau, The Gambia, Haiti, India, Indonesia, Iran, Iraq, Ivory Coast, Jordan, Kazakhstan, Kirgizstan, Korea (North), Laos, Lebanon, Liberia, Libya, Macedonia, Madagascar, Mali, Mauritania, Moldova, Mongolia, Morocco, Mozambique, Nepal, Nigeria, Oman, Pakistan, Philippines, Romania, Russia, Rwanda, São Tomé and Príncipe, Saudi Arabia, Senegal, Sierra Leone, Somalia, Sri Lanka, Sudan, Syria, Taiwan, Thailand, Tajikistan, Tanzania, Togo, Tunisia, Turkey, Turkmenistan, Uganda, Ukraine, Uzbekistan, Vietnam, Yemen, Zaire, the territories formerly comprising the Socialist Federal Republic of Yugoslavia, excluding Croatia and Slovenia.

You will also require a visa if you come into any of the following categories:

- persons holding passports or travel documents issued by the former Soviet Union or by the former Socialist Federal Republic of Yugoslavia;
- stateless persons;
- persons holding non-national documents.

Non-visa nationals
Non-visa nationals are those people who do not need to obtain a visa to enter the UK. If you are a non-visa national, you are not required to obtain any form of entry clearance prior to arriving in the UK but if you are planning to stay for longer than six months, it is advisable to obtain either an entry certificate or a letter of consent. If you have either of these forms of entry clearance, your entry through immigration will be easier if you encounter any problems. If you are refused entry into the UK as a student, and you do not have any form of entry clearance, then you will have no right of appeal in the UK against this decision. If you do have entry clearance you will be allowed temporary admission in order to make an appeal.

Obtaining entry clearance (visa or entry certificate)
In order to obtain any form of entry clearance, you should contact your local British Embassy, British High Commission or Consulate.
There is a charge for all types of entry clearance. This is currently:

- single entry visa: £16.50 if you are under twenty-five years of age or £33 if you are over twenty-five.

- multiple-entry visa: £45.

A multiple-entry visa is recommended for visa nationals who are planning to enrol on a course which will last for less than six months and who intend to leave and re-enter the UK.

When you apply for any form of entry clearance you need to prove that you meet the requirements of the UK immigration regulations which relate to students. These are as follows:

- that you have been accepted on to a full-time course of study at a genuine education institution (full-time degree course or any other course involving a minimum of fifteen hours' per week organized daytime study of a single or related subjects);
- that you can meet the cost of your course fees and your living expenses and those of any family you may be bringing with you, without working and without claiming state benefit;
- that you have the required qualifications or level of training for the course you intend to take;
- that you intend to leave the UK at the end of the course.

ℹ Regulations regarding student nurses and postgraduate doctors and dentists are slightly different and if this applies to you, you are advised to obtain details from your local British Council Office, or from the British Embassy, High Commission or Consulate.

If you are an EEA national you may study in Britain and you have the right of residence for the duration of the course of study, but your residence permit needs to be renewed annually. You do not have the right to permanent residence. As an EEA student you are also free to take employment or to be self-employed. You are not able to claim public funds and you have no automatic right to payment of maintenance grants. Different rules apply to part-time students who are also seeking work, but here we are concerned with full-time students.

The EEA contracting party states are: Austria, Belgium, Denmark, Finland, France, Germany, Greece, Iceland, Ireland, Italy, Luxembourg, the Netherlands, Norway, Portugal, Spain, Sweden, United Kingdom.

Requirements for student status: all categories

If you enter Britain as an international student you are required to be able to accommodate and support yourself, and your dependants, without needing any public funds. Such public funds include:

- income support;
- family credit;
- housing benefit;
- housing as a homeless person;
- council tax benefit.

If you do make any claim for such funds, you could endanger your future immigration status in the UK.

To claim student status, you will have to have proof of acceptance for a course of study at:

- a publicly-funded institution of further or higher education;
- a bona fide private education institution which maintains satisfactory records of enrolment and attendance;
- an independent fee-paying school outside the maintained sector.

You will have to be able to follow:

- a recognized full-time degree at a publicly-funded institution of further education or higher education; or
- a weekday full-time course involving attendance at a single institution for a minimum of fifteen hours' organized daytime study of a single subject or directly related subjects; or
- a full-time course of study at an independent fee-paying school.

You must also intend to leave Britain at the end of your studies; you must not intend to engage in business or take employment, except part-time or vacation work undertaken with the consent of the Secretary of State for Employment, and you must be able to meet the costs of your course, accommodation and maintenance without recourse to public funds.

Similar conditions for entry apply to student nurses, but acceptable courses are defined as those meeting the requirements of the UK Central Council for Nursing, Midwifery and Health Visiting.

Acceptance on a course must not be obtained by misrepresentation.

Postgraduate doctors or dentists must be graduates of a UK medical school intending to undertake Pre-Registration House Officer employment for up to twelve months, as required for full registration with the General Medical Council. They must not have spent more than twelve months in aggregate in Pre-Registration House Officer employment, or they must be doctors or dentists eligible for full or limited registration with the General Medical Council or the General Dental Council who intend to undertake postgraduate training in a hospital and who have not spent more than four years in aggregate in the UK as a doctor or dentist (excluding any period spent in Pre-Registration House Officer employment). They must intend to leave the UK on completing their training.

Registration with the police

The stamp which will be put into your passport on entering the UK will state whether or not you are required to register with the police. EEA nationals and Commonwealth citizens will not be required to register. If you are from any other country, aged over sixteen and intending to stay in the UK for more than six months, then it is likely that you will be required to register with the police. Anyone entering the UK as your dependant may also be required to register.

If you are required to register, then you must do so within seven days of arrival in the UK. In order to register you need to take your passport, two photographs of yourself and the registration fee (currently £30) to your local police station. If you are studying in London, you should go to the Aliens' Registration Office (see address at end of this chapter). After this, each time you change your address and whenever you extend your leave to remain in the UK, you must renew your police registration. There is no charge for this unless you have lost your registration document.

Prospective students

If you wish to enter the UK as a prospective student before enrolling on a specific course of study, you will need to:

- demonstrate a genuine and realistic intention of undertaking, within six months of your date of entry, a course of study which would meet the requirements for entry (or extension of stay) as a student;

- show that you intend to leave the UK on completion of your studies (or expiry of your leave to enter);
- prove that you can meet the costs of your prospective course, accommodation and maintenance without recourse to public funds.

If you wish to enter the UK as a prospective student, you may be given leave to do so for six months, provided you can satisfy the conditions above.

Spouses and dependants

Your spouse (your husband or wife) may be allowed to enter the UK provided:

- you have been given leave to enter the UK as a student;
- you and your spouse intend to live with each other as husband and wife during your stay;
- there will be adequate accommodation for you and your spouse and any dependants without recourse to public funds;
- you and your spouse will be able to maintain yourselves and any dependants without recourse to public funds;
- you or your spouse do not intend to work unless specifically given permission to do so;
- you or your spouse intend to leave the UK at the end of the period of leave granted.

Your dependants may also be allowed to enter the UK if:

- they are under eighteen or have current leave to enter;
- they are unmarried and have not formed an independent family unit and are not leading an independent life;
- they can and will be maintained and accommodated without recourse to public funds;
- they will not stay in the UK beyond the period of leave granted to the parent.

More detailed information on rights and responsibilities for international students, and their spouses and families (e.g. access to benefits, state schooling, employment, rights for spouses) is available from UKCOSA (address at the end of this chapter).

3.2   Extending your leave to remain in the UK

It is important to note the date which is stamped in your passport when you pass through immigration control. This is the date when your current leave to remain (permission to stay in the UK) will expire. By this date your should either leave the UK, or extend your leave to remain.

Most international students will be given one year's leave to remain in the first instance, unless you are sponsored by your own government or another official sponsor, in which case you may be given leave to remain for the entire length of your course.

How to extend your leave to remain

If you need to stay longer than the period you are originally given then you will need to apply for an extension of your leave to remain. You should make this application about eight weeks before your current leave to remain expires, that is, eight weeks before the date stamped in your passport. To apply, you need to take or send the documents listed below to the Home Office.

To extend your permission to remain you need to complete an application form available from the Home Office Immigration and Nationality Department (IND) or one of the Public Enquiry Offices (PEOs) (the addresses for these and the Home Office are at the end of this chapter). The form gives details of what documents you need to send in support of your application, and will include:

- your passport or travel document;
- your police registration certificate (if you have one);
- a letter from your college or university stating that you are still enrolled on a full-time course of study or due to begin another one;
- a bank statement or other evidence that you have enough money to continue to pay your fees and maintain yourself and any dependants;
- a letter from yourself listing the documents that you have enclosed and requesting an extension of your leave to remain as a student.

If you are sending these documents by post, you should send them by Recorded Delivery and also keep a photocopy of everything you send. You can expect to wait at least four weeks before you receive any reply.

If, for any reason, you do not have all these documents available, do not delay making your application. You must still make your application before your current leave to remain expires but in this case you should enclose as many of the documents as you have and also a letter explaining what is missing, why it is missing and when you expect to be able to forward it to the Home Office.

What you should do if your application is refused
If your application for extension of leave to remain is refused, you will receive a letter from the Home Office telling you why it has been refused. The letter will also tell you whether or not you have the right to appeal against the decision. If you had made your original application in good time, that is before your current leave to remain had expired, then you should automatically be given the right to appeal. However, your appeal must be made within fourteen days. Making an appeal is not a straightforward process and if this happens to you, you must seek professional advice. If this is necessary you should go to either:

- a student adviser or welfare officer at your college or university;
- your university or college students' union;
- the Immigration Appeals Advisory Service (address at end of this chapter);
- the UK Council for International Education (UKCOSA) (address at end of this chapter).

Late applications
There may be a valid reason why you have to make a late application for an extension of your leave to remain. If this is the case you must contact one of the people or organizations listed above and they will help you with your application. If you do have to make a late application, and this application is refused, then you do not have the right of appeal against this decision.

3.3 Students and employment

Students wishing to work while they study are not normally allowed to do so except on a very restricted basis, and you should not depend on being able to work in order to help pay for your course or your living expenses.

However, some international students may be allowed to take certain types of employment provided that:

- the stamp in your passport does not prohibit you from applying for a work permit;
- there is no suitable resident worker available to fill the post;
- the work will not interfere with your studies.

Students from the EEA do not need to obtain permission to work but if you are from a country outside the EEA then you will need to obtain a work permit before taking up any kind of employment.

What types of work can you do?

As an international student, there are limited types of work that you can do. These are listed below, along with the procedures for obtaining the relevant work permit. Never begin work until you have obtained your work permit.

Part-time and vacation work

Students may be given permission to take part-time work (for a maximum of twenty hours per week during term-time) or work during the vacations. You have to find a job before you can apply for a work permit and you must apply for a new work permit each time you change jobs. To apply you should:

- take your passport and police registration certificate (if you have one) to your local Jobcentre (you can find their address by looking in the telephone directory under 'Employment Service – Jobcentres');
- ask for form OSSI;
- complete part 1 of the form yourself, ask your employer to complete part 2 and take part 3 to be completed by someone at your college or university;
- take the completed form back to the Jobcentre.

When permission to work is granted, the work permit will be sent to your employer.

It can be very difficult to find work and permission will be given only if there is no one from the local work-force suitable for the job.

Work experience during your course

If practical work experience is required as part of your course, the college or university must normally apply for a work permit for all the students on the course. It is important to check with the college or university that the work experience programme is approved by the Department for Education and Employment.

Practical training or work experience at the end of your course

Practical training and work experience are two separate categories and although they are applied for in the same way, you cannot transfer your permit from one to the other. Training of a practical nature is what might be required by someone seeking a professional qualification in an area such as accountancy, architecture or engineering. The period of training required must be agreed in advance and you have to agree to return home once the training is complete. Work experience at the end of your course might be permitted for a maximum of twelve months.

The procedure for obtaining a permit to take either training or work experience is as follows:

- Contact the Department for Education and Employment (address at the end of this chapter) to obtain form WP2.
- Ask your prospective employer to complete the form and return it to the Department for Education and Employment.

It will take at least eight weeks for a reply to your application.

Special arrangements are available for nurses, doctors and dentists to work after they have qualified or while they are undertaking training, provided that the work experience is a necessary step to becoming qualified. Again, check the situation with the college or university concerned.

Postgraduate research assistants

Postgraduate research students may take teaching and demonstration work in laboratories without obtaining permission from the Department for Education and Employment provided that the work does not exceed six hours per week.

National Insurance and tax

Students from overseas who are working in the UK must pay National Insurance (NI) contributions. It is your responsibility to apply for a NI number before you start work. You should obtain an application form from your local National Insurance Contributions Department (look up 'Contributions Agency' in your telephone directory). You may have to wait at least ten weeks before you are allocated a NI number, but you can start work as soon as you have submitted your application.

You will automatically be subject to UK taxation rules.

3.4   Checklists

Official documentation you will require in order to enter the UK

Students from the EEA
✓ valid passport or national identity card.

Students from outside the EEA
✓ passport;
✓ a valid visa or entry certificate;
✓ proof of financial support;
✓ letter of acceptance from school, college or university.

Student nurses
✓ all documents listed above; plus
✓ medical certificate.

Official documentation you may require during your stay in Britain
✓ unexpired leave to remain in the UK;
✓ police registration certificate;
✓ work permit (if working);
✓ National Insurance number (if working).

3.5   Sources of information

Addresses of organizations mentioned in this chapter
Aliens' Registration Office, 10 Lambs Conduit Street, London WC1X 3MX,

Tel: (0)171-230 1208 (open: 9.00 a.m.– 4.45 p.m., Monday–Friday).

Department for Education and Employment, Overseas Labour Section, Block C, Porter Brook House, Moorfoot, Sheffield S1 4PQ, Tel: (0)1742 753275 (24-hour service for work permit application forms: (0) 1272 244780).

Immigration Appeals Advisory Service, 3rd Floor, County House, 190 Great Dover Street, London SE1 4YB, Tel: (0)171-357 7511.

Immigration and Nationality Department, Home Office, Lunar House, 40 Wellesley Road, Croydon CR9 2BY, Tel: (0)181-686 0688.

Regional Public Enquiries Offices
Belfast: Immigration Office, Olive Tree House, Fountain Street, Belfast BT1 5EA, Tel: (0)1232 322547.

Birmingham: Immigration Office (Cargo Terminal), Birmingham Airport, Birmingham B26 3QN, Tel: (0)121-782 3600.

Glasgow: Immigration Office, Admin. Block D, Argyll Avenue, Glasgow Airport, Paisley PA3 2T, Tel: (0)141-887 2255.

Harwich: Immigration Office, Parkeston Quay, Harwich CO12 4SX, Tel: (0)1255 504371.

Liverpool: Immigration Office, Graeme House, Derby Square, Liverpool L2 7SF, Tel: (0)151-236 8974.

Norwich: Immigration Office, Norwich Airport, Fifers Lane, Norwich NR6 6EP, Tel: (0)1603 408859.

UKCOSA: The Council for International Education, 9–17 St Albans Place, London N1 0NX, Tel: (0)171-226 3762 (telephone advice service available 1.00–4.00 p.m., Monday–Friday: Tel. 0171-354 5210).

Further reading
UKCOSA sheets: *Changing status and staying in the UK; Council Tax and the international student; International students, their families and marriage; Students and immigration (after arrival in the UK); Students and employment* (available from your local British Council office).

4   Arriving in Britain

In this chapter we tell you what to expect and what to do when you
arrive at a major airport, seaport or railway terminal.

4.1   Immigration control

When you arrive in Britain, whether it is by air or sea, the first thing
you will have to do is to go through passport control. You will find
that there are two different queues of people going through passport
control:

- EU and EEA nationals;
- all other passport holders.

Make sure that you join the right queue or you could waste a lot of
time. When you reach immigration control you should have all your
documents ready and be prepared to answer questions about yourself
and what you intend to do during your stay in the UK.

You may be asked to undergo a routine health check by the airport
doctor. If this happens, remember that it is merely a formality and
that after the health check you should go back to immigration
control.

Problems at immigration
Hopefully you will pass through immigration without encountering
any problems but if you do have problems you should either:

- ask the Immigration Officer to telephone your college or
  university; or
- ask to see a representative of the Immigration Appeals Advisory
  Service.

They can be contacted on one of the following numbers, depending
on which airport or seaport you are at:

- From Heathrow Airport: 759 9234
- From Gatwick Airport: 533385

- From Manchester Airport: 834 9942
- From Birmingham Airport: 706 9765
- From Dover East (seaport):   240 1234
- From Dover West (seaport):   240 2461

4.2   Customs control

Once you have collected your luggage, you will then have to pass through customs control. You will normally have a choice of three different channels:

- the blue channel – if you are travelling from the EU;
- the green channel – if you are travelling from outside the EU and have nothing to declare;
- the red channel – if you are travelling from outside the EU but have goods to declare.

ⓘ If you are carrying more than your permitted allowance of duty-free or tax-free goods, or any prohibited goods, then you must pass through the red channel. If you are unsure about what you are allowed to bring into the UK, check with your local British Embassy, High Commission or Consulate before leaving your home country. Even if you have nothing to declare and go through the green channel, you may still be stopped and asked to open your luggage.

4.3   Onward travel

Many students arrange their onward travel with their travel agents when they make their flight arrangements. If this is what you have done, then you can carry out the next stage of your journey by following the instructions you have already been given or by finding out what to do next by showing your travel documents at the information desk in the airport or seaport. If your visit has been arranged by the British Council, your local Council office will advise
ⓘ you about your onward journey. If you are making independent arrangements for onward travel, then it will help you to obtain information from your place of study about the best way to travel from your point of entry. The British Tourist Authority should also be able to provide you with travel information if you contact them well in advance of coming to Britain. If you cannot do any of these

things, then the general information desk at the airport or seaport will have someone to advise you of the best way to reach your final destination.

For many of you, your first experience of travel in Britain will be from Heathrow or Gatwick airports to central London. Your final destination may be in London itself or you may be travelling from one of London's many coach or railway stations to another part of Britain. If you have arrived at one of Britain's other airports, you may be able to travel directly to your destination.

Travel from Gatwick airport

After landing, allow about two hours to reach central London. The easiest way is to take an overground (British Rail) train to Victoria main-line station. From there you can transfer to the London Underground system. If your final destination is not London, you may be able to avoid travelling into central London and take a bus or train directly from Gatwick. The cities of Birmingham, Manchester, Brighton, Reading and Liverpool, for example, can all be reached directly from Gatwick airport.

Travel from Heathrow airport

The quickest way of getting to central London from Heathrow is by underground, commonly known as 'the tube'. The journey takes approximately forty-five minutes and currently costs £3.10. Trains run every five minutes from 5.00 a.m. until 11.45 p.m., Monday to Saturday and from 6.45 a.m. to 11.00 p.m. on Sundays.

Another way of getting to central London from Heathrow is the bus. Although this will take longer (between one and one-and-a-half hours) it can be easier if you are carrying a lot of luggage. There are two buses – Airbus A1 which goes to Victoria main-line railway station, and Airbus A2 which goes to Euston main-line railway station. There is also a bus which will take you to Gatwick or Luton airports if you have a connecting flight. If your final destination is not London and you wish to avoid travelling through central London, you can take a bus from Heathrow airport to Reading railway station (approximately one hour) and from there catch a train to a variety of destinations including Bath, Birmingham, Bristol, Cardiff, Exeter, Oxford, Plymouth, Southampton and Swansea.

Using the underground

The underground system in London has eleven different lines, each of which has a name and is shown in a different colour on the underground map (see inside back cover).

Heathrow airport is on the Piccadilly line which is dark blue on the map. If your destination is not on the Piccadilly line then you will have to change lines at some point during your journey. You do this by getting off the train at the station where the line you need crosses the line you are travelling on, then follow the signs for the line you want.

Before you can enter the underground you need to buy a ticket. To do this, you need to know the name of the station you are travelling to. You can buy a ticket from either one of the automatic machines or the ticket office. Once you have bought your ticket you normally enter the underground by going through an automatic gate. This can be quite difficult if you are carrying a lot of bulky luggage. Because of this the automatic gate system is not used at Heathrow; however you will find automatic gates at your destination. If you do have a lot of luggage then you should ask one of the attendants to let you through a special gate. When you are using the automatic gates, you use your ticket to operate the gate by putting it into the slot. Don't forget to pick up your ticket at the other side of the gate as you will need it again when you leave the underground.

Most underground stations have long escalators (moving stairways) which take you to and from the trains. These can be quite challenging if you have a lot of luggage. If you can, try to keep yourself and your luggage to the right-hand side of the escalator, leaving space for people in a hurry to walk past you on the left.

Taxis

Taking a taxi from any of London's airports into central London is a very expensive option, although if there is a group of three or four of you together with a lot of luggage then you may feel that it would be worthwhile taking a taxi. A taxi from Heathrow to central London will cost a minimum of £35. If you have arrived at one of Britain's regional airports it may be less expensive to take a taxi to your final destination (around £10–£20). If your college or university has not provided you with details of travel from a local airport then you should contact them and ask for the information. In any case, you should always ask the taxi driver what will be the approximate cost of the journey before you start.

Travel from London to other destinations in Britain

If you have arrived in London but your final destination is outside London, you will probably be continuing your journey from one of London's main-line railway stations or coach stations. Train travel is quickest, but more expensive than travel by coach or bus.

Travel by train

The fare structure for rail travel is quite complicated and varies according to when you are travelling and how far in advance you book your ticket. You may find that a travel agent in your home country can include your rail travel as part of your complete travel package. However, if you are booking your own rail ticket you would be well advised to book in advance using a credit card, if you have one. This means that you can obtain something called an Apex fare. Apex and Super Apex fares have to be bought at least one week in advance of travelling (or at least two weeks in advance for Super Apex). You have to travel on a specified train and if you have to change your travel plans, you will be charged a supplement. In order to book an Apex ticket, you need to phone one of the stations listed below. Each of London's railway stations serves a different part of Britain: check below to see which station you will need. Use the general phone number for information about fare and times and the credit-card booking number, where given, to make an advance booking.

Destination	London station	Telephone numbers
❶ Birmingham, Blackpool, Carlisle, Chester, Coventry, Glasgow, Lancaster, Liverpool, Manchester, Preston	Euston	*General information* (0)171-387 7070 *Credit-card booking* (0)171-387 8541

Destination	London station	Telephone numbers
❶ Aberdeen, Cambridge, Derby, Edinburgh, Hull, Leeds, Leicester, Loughborough, Newcastle, Nottingham, Sheffield, York	Kings Cross and St Pancras	*General information* (0)171-278 2477 *Credit-card booking* (0)171-278 9431
Bath, Bristol, Cardiff, Exeter, Oxford, Penzance, Plymouth, Reading, Swansea	Paddington	*General information* (0)171-262 6767
Bournemouth, Portsmouth, Salisbury, Southampton, Weymouth, Winchester	Waterloo	*General information* (0)171-928 5100 *Credit-card booking* (0)171-620 1032
Canterbury, Dover, Margate, Ramsgate	Charing Cross	*General information* (0)171-928 5100 *Credit-card booking* (0)171-620 1032
Brighton, Eastbourne, Gatwick, Maidstone, Worthing	Victoria	*General information* (0)171-928 5100 *Credit-card booking* (0)171-620 1032

Travel by coach

Most coaches leaving London will depart from Victoria Coach
Station, which is approximately ten minutes' walk from Victoria
railway station. There are a variety of different coach operators, and
therefore a wide variety of fares and timetables. One major coach
company which operates throughout Britain is National Express.
ⓘ For details of fares, timetables and credit card booking you can
phone (0)171-730 0202.

Some examples of fares from London by rail and by coach are given
below. These are standard single (one way) weekday fares. You can
expect to pay more at weekends and during peak travel hours.

	Rail	Coach
London–Edinburgh	£59.00	£20.00
London–Oxford	£12.30	£ 6.20
London–Bristol	£25.00	£17.50
London–Leeds	£44.00	£12.00
London–Manchester	£50.00	£19.00
London–Swansea	£30.50	£23.50

4.4   Short-term accommodation

If you need to stay overnight or for one or two days near the airport
or in London before going on to your destination, there are a number
of options you might consider.

● You can make arrangements in advance if you write to the
  London Tourist Board at least six weeks before your visit. They
  will make a provisional booking for you and will confirm the
  arrangement in writing.
● If there is a British Tourist Authority Office in your own country,
  they can help you make an advance booking.
● If your place of study is part of the British Council's Meeting
  and Greeting Service, a Council representative will help you
  make arrangements when you arrive. Details of what to do will be
  sent to you by your college or university.
● You will find help at the information desks of airports and
  seaports.

ⓘ You should expect to pay an average of £50 per night for bed and breakfast in a medium-range London hotel and £30 per night in a guest house. However, there is a great variation in prices according to the area and the season, as well the degree of luxury on offer.

4.5　What to expect on arrival

Arrival in a foreign country is usually a disorienting experience and it is helpful to be aware of the factors that will influence the way you feel when you step off the aeroplane or leave the ship or train.

Climate

If you are making a long-haul journey, then it is important to remember that you may be facing a very different climate when you arrive in Britain. It is a good idea to find out in advance what the current temperatures and weather patterns are so that you can carry the appropriate clothing with you. The weather in Britain is very unpredictable and it can often be wet and cold even in summer, so one item of warm clothing and a raincoat and umbrella are probably a sensible precaution no matter when you arrive.

'The weather in Britain is very unpredictable'

Time difference

Before you leave, make sure you know what the time will be in Britain on your arrival. This is important particularly if you have a long journey to make from your point of entry. If you arrive very late at night onward transport might be more difficult to arrange and you may wish to consider spending a night in a hotel near the airport.

The best time to arrive is on a weekday (Monday, Tuesday, Wednesday, Thursday, or Friday) and not during the weekend or on a public holiday. Most offices and many shops and other facilities will be closed at the weekend, particularly on a Sunday, and trains and buses will be less frequent. Also try to arrive during office hours (9.00 a.m.–5.00 p.m.) if possible, just in case you have any problems and require professional advice. The ideal time to arrive is in the morning. This gives you plenty of time to reach your final destination and settle in.

Security on arrival

Airports, seaports and stations are usually busy places and it is important to be careful to protect your money, documents and luggage when you arrive. Britain is no more dangerous or threatening than any other European country, but all major airports, stations and seaports in big cities are places where the traveller is vulnerable.

Documents

Take special care of your passport, travel documents and tickets, but keep a separate note of your passport number and its date and place of issue. If you have this information, it will be easier for a replacement to be made. If you do lose your passport inform the police and your Embassy immediately.

Money, cash cards and credit cards, travellers' cheques

Try not to carry large sums of cash with you. Travellers are an easy target for thieves and if cash is stolen it is almost impossible to trace. Bring only enough for small immediate needs (£30–£50): you can buy rail tickets and pay hotel bills by credit card, for example. Keep cash, cash cards and credit cards in a safe place (e.g. an inside pocket, a money belt round your waist, or a handbag, not in a back trouser pocket). Keep a record of travellers' cheque serial numbers so that you can inform your bank if they are lost. Report any loss or theft to the police immediately and inform your bank if you lose cash cards or credit cards.

Handbags and luggage
Never leave you luggage unattended. Think about wearing a money belt. Valuable items should not be packed in your main luggage but kept with you in your hand luggage. In general it is better not to bring many valuables such as jewellery with you. Label your luggage so it can be more easily traced if 'lost in transit'. If you need to deposit your luggage when you arrive, while you change money, make telephone calls, etc., then find an official 'left luggage' office. You will be given a receipt so that you can reclaim your luggage later and it will be properly supervised. A small charge will be made for each item of luggage left.

Any luggage which is lost in transit should be reported immediately to the officials of the air or shipping line. If you lose items at the airport, seaport or station then go to the 'lost property office' to see if anyone has handed them in. If you lose luggage in any other way, or think it has been stolen, then report the matter at once to the police.

4.6   Sources of information

Addresses of organizations mentioned in this chapter
The London Tourist Board, 26 Grosvenor Gardens, London SW1W 0DU, Tel: (0)171-730 3450 (also has offices at Victoria Station, London; Liverpool Street Station, London; Heathrow Airport, Terminals 1, 2 and 3).

British Tourist Authority, Thames Tower, Black's Road, London W6 9EL, Tel: (0)181-846 9000.

5 Accommodation

In this chapter we examine the range of accommodation available, its costs and how to make your arrangements.

5.1 Arrangements to make before you leave

It is advisable to make your arrangements for long-term accommodation before you arrive. This is normally done through the accommodation office at your place of study. Universities and many colleges of higher education have halls of residence which give priority to first-year students and international students. Even if you wish eventually to find independent (private) accommodation, halls of residence offer many advantages for new arrivals to Britain. You will be close to fellow students as well as to your place of study and you will have an opportunity to become familiar with the area and the other types of accommodation available while you are settling in.

You will be sent a form to fill in when you receive the offer of a place on your course. Make sure you complete the form fully and return it by the date specified.

Even if your institution does not have residential accommodation, there will almost certainly be an accommodation office that can help you arrange your accommodation before you arrive. You are strongly advised to use this service as it will be expensive to stay in short-term accommodation while you try to find your own accommodation once you arrive.

5.2 Types of accommodation available

University or college accommodation
This can include halls of residence, college or university-owned houses for small communities of single students, and flats for married students. Meals may be provided but most accommodation is now self-catering. This accommodation should be booked when you enrol on your course and priority is given to first-year students. For information contact the university or college accommodation officer. Average costs may be around £44–£55 per week.

'Halls of residence ... give priority to international students'

Student hostels

Privately run hostels provide rooms for single and (only occasionally) married students. Many provide meals but some have self-catering facilities. Some are for nationals of specific countries: others are specifically for international students of all nationalities. You need to apply direct to the hostel to make a booking (addresses are given in Appendix 2). Average costs are from £45 per week.

Lodgings/host family accommodation

Living in lodgings means renting accommodation in someone else's home. It may be the home of a family with children, a young or elderly couple or a single person. This type of accommodation may not offer you as much freedom as you would like (you may have to alter your lifestyle to fit in with your host) but it does mean that you will have some company. It can almost feel like being at home – except that you are living with a different family. In some cases, meals will be included, or otherwise you may have the use of the household kitchen to prepare your own meals. Average costs vary from approximately £35–£70 per week, depending on the range of services offered. Your college accommodation office may be able to find accommodation for you, with a host family, otherwise you can look for advertisements in local newspapers and on shop or college notice-boards.

Bedsits

Larger houses are often divided into units called bedsits which are rented out to couples or individuals. A bedsit is normally one room which contains living, sleeping and sometimes even cooking facilities. If the cooking facilities are not in your main room then it is likely that you will have to share them with other people renting bedsits in the same house. Sometimes the owner of the property also lives on the premises. This type of accommodation give you plenty of freedom but, on the other hand, can make you feel very isolated.

Rented flats and houses

Self-contained, furnished flats and houses are more expensive to rent and can be difficult to find, although the situation varies enormously across the country. When you rent on this basis you normally have to sign a legal agreement with the landlord (a lease) and you may have to pay an initial deposit as security against any breakages or damage (see sections 5.3 and 5.4 below). Again, the accommodation officer in your place of study will be able to advise you about the availability of such accommodation and how to find it. These rentals are also advertised locally. Costs depend on size and location of the accommodation.

Youth hostels

Youth hostels provide inexpensive and usually very basic accommodation, mainly for tourists and sightseers on a tight budget. The accommodation is essentially short-term. More information about how to make use of youth hostels is given in Chapter 9. Typical cost, per night, is £8.

5.3   Housing agreements and your rights

If you decide to look for a flat or house to rent, you will need to sign a written agreement between yourself, as tenant, and the landlord. Tenants and landlords have certain rights protected by law, but you must check the agreement before you sign in case you think there is something unreasonable in it.

If you have problems with accommodation, contact the accommodation officer or the students' union at your place of study. Should the problem be of a more legal nature, then the local Citizens Advice Bureau will be able to tell you your rights as a tenant and the rights of your landlord.

5.4   Checklist – points to consider when renting private accommodation

- ✅ What does the rent cover: meals, electricity, gas, hot water; use of telephone, television?
- ✅ When is rent to be paid?
- ✅ How will you keep a record of what you have paid – is there a rent book, for example?
- ✅ Are there any meters for gas, electricity, telephone? If so, how much will you pay per unit?
- ✅ If you pay an initial deposit, when will this be returned?
- ✅ Ensure that the initial deposit being requested is no more than two months' rent.
- ✅ Ensure that you have a receipt for the initial deposit.
- ✅ How long is your lease?
- ✅ If you are renting a flat or house, will you or your spouse be responsible for paying the Council Tax? If so, check to see how much this will add to your outgoings. (Normally full-time students and the non-British spouses of international students are exempt from paying this tax, but spouses may be liable.)
- ✅ If you wish to stop the agreement, on what terms can you do so?
- ✅ If you wish to leave the accommodation, what period of notice must you give the landlord?
- ✅ If the landlord wishes you to leave, how much notice must he give you?

5.5   Sources of information

Further reading
UKCOSA sheet: *Accommodation* (available from your local British Council office)

6   Financial and legal matters

In this chapter we provide information about the costs of studying
and living in Britain and managing your money.

6.1   Fees and the costs of study

It is possible to give you only a rough estimate of the amount of
money you will need for your stay, but of course there are variations
in costs across the country and variations in the needs of different
individuals.

Before you come to Britain you need to:

- calculate how much money you think you will need;
- know what your sources of money will be;
- arrange a method of transferring money from your own country
  to Britain.

The majority of international students coming to study in Britain
will be asked to pay the overseas fee. Unless you are a national of an
EU country, in order to qualify for home-fee status you must satisfy
the following conditions:

- You must have been ordinarily resident in the UK for a full three
years before 1 September or 1 January of the year your course
begins. 'Ordinarily resident' means that you are living in the UK on
a settled basis and not temporarily – as a student or a visitor, for
example.
- At no time during that three-year period were you in the UK
wholly or mainly for the purpose of receiving full-time education.
One exception to this residence requirement concerns those who
have been granted settled status in the UK. Anyone who has become
a British citizen or has been given the right to settle in the UK
within the three-year period prior to the start of their course and
who has taken up residence in the UK by a specified date (either 1
January, 1 April or 1 September prior to the start of the course) will
be entitled to pay the home-rate fee.

If you are a national of an EU country, you will qualify for home-fee status if you satisfy the following conditions:

- You must have been ordinarily resident in the European Economic Area (EEA) for three years immediately preceding the 1 September, 1 January or 1 April closest to the beginning of your course.
- The purpose of your residence was not wholly or mainly to take up full-time education.

An exception to this rule exists for anyone who was not resident in the EEA for the specified three-year period only because they, their parents or spouse were temporarily employed outside the EEA.

ⓘ There are further exceptions to the three-year rules both for EU and non-EU students. If you are in doubt about fees or think that you may have been charged the wrong rate of fee, you should contact your local British Council office if you are still overseas or, if you are already in Britain, the welfare officer or students' union at your place of study.

6.2   Scholarships and funding

If you wish to find out whether you are eligible for any funding for your course of study, you should make initial enquiries in your home country. Your own Ministry or Department of Education is the starting-point for such enquiries. You will also find information sheets at your local British Council office giving details of awards available.

Awards are not normally available for study at undergraduate level, although EEA students who satisfy the conditions for 'home' fee status may be eligible for a fee-only award from the British government. You should ask your institution about how to apply for such an award.

The eligibility requirements for most grants and scholarships are absolutely precise and unless you meet the criteria in respect of age, sex, nationality and subject of study, your application will not be considered. It is vital that you are sure you have funds to cover your course fees and cost of living before coming to Britain because you will be unable to arrange financial support once you have left you home country.

The following are some of the scholarship schemes available for students from overseas.

British Council fellowships for postgraduate study or research
The fellowships are awarded by the British Council Director overseas and you have to apply to your local British Council office. The funding ranges from small grants for short periods of study to fully-funded awards for fees and living expenses.

Commonwealth scholarships
Offered to citizens of Commonwealth countries or British dependent territories. You normally have to be under thirty-five and permanently resident in those areas. These awards are primarily for postgraduate study, although funding for a first degree may be considered if there are no suitable undergraduate courses available at home. Apply to the Commonwealth Scholarship Agency in your home country.

Chevening awards
These awards are normally made for courses at postgraduate level and preference is given to candidates already established in a career. They are granted to particularly able students from countries with whom Britain's economic relations are expected to develop. You should enquire at the British Embassy, High Commission or British Council office in your home country.

ODA Shared Scholarships (ODASS)
These scholarships are jointly funded by the Overseas Development Administration and certain British higher education institutions. They are normally given for taught postgraduate courses. To be eligible, you must be from a developing Commonwealth country and not be employed by your government. You can obtain a list of institutions participating from the British High Commission or your local British Council office. Applications should then be made directly to the institution concerned.

Overseas Research Student Awards Scheme (ORSAS)
These are for postgraduate study and are awarded on a competitive basis. They are initially for one year and make up the difference between 'home' and 'overseas' students fees. Application forms are available from the British higher education institution at which you wish to study.

6.3   Costs of living

The cost-of-living guide below is only a rough estimate and does not take into account the extra costs involved in bringing members of your family with you. Prices vary a great deal from one area to another and London prices will probably be higher than those given here. Remember too to enquire at your students' union to find out what special reductions are available for students at local shops, theatres, cinemas, museums and galleries, and also special student fares on buses and trains.

💷 **Approximate cost of living for twelve months including accommodation, heating and lighting, food and daily travel (based on 1994–95 prices)**
- London £7,500;
- elsewhere in the UK £5,000–£6,500.

Additional expenses
- books £300–£700;
- clothing £400–£500;

- deposit on rented accommodation £250–£400 (equivalent of one month's rent);
- short-term accommodation £3–£50 per night.

Items of clothing

The prices below give you an approximate idea of what you would need to spend to buy goods of a reasonable quality in typical high-street chain stores in Britain. It is, of course, possible to find cheaper items at certain discount stores and street markets, or if you are prepared to accept a lower quality. At the other end of the scale, extra high-quality and fashion items are available if you can afford to pay considerably more.

£ *£10 and under:* T-shirts, items of underwear such as socks, pants, vests (women's tights and stockings can be bought from £1.50).
£20 and under: shirts, blouses, light shoes and sandals, light sweaters for men and women, nightclothes, summer dresses and skirts for women.
£30 and under: trousers, jeans, skirts, heavier shoes for women, light jackets for women, heavier weight sweaters for men and women.
£50 and under: women's raincoats, women's boots, warm jackets for men and women, warm trousers for men.
£90 and under: men's raincoats, men's and women's winter coats.

Other costs to consider

£
- *Heat and light* (if not included in accommodation charge): allow £20 – £30 per week in winter; £5 per week in summer.
- *Food* (if not included in accommodation charge): allow £50 per week.
- *Books:* textbooks will vary in price enormously from about £10 to £50 and over, but some may be available second-hand. Light reading material is available in paperback editions with prices around £5, but second-hand books can be bought for under £1.
- *Newspapers:* 25p – 45p daily.
- *Launderette:* £1.50 – £2.50.
- *Magazines:* 50p – £2.50.
- *Soap:* 50p per bar minimum.
- *Toothpaste:* £1.50 on average for a medium-sized tube.
- *Shampoo:* prices start from about £1.
- *Condoms:* £1 for 5.
- *Cigarettes:* £2.50 upwards per packet of 20.

- *Hairdresser:* wash and cut for men: £10; for women: £12–£20.
- *Dry cleaning:* £4 for skirt or trousers; £8 for heavy coat.
- *A restaurant meal:* £5 per head minimum; £12 per head average (drinks extra).
- *Wine:* table wine is available for approximately £2.50 for a 75cl bottle.
- *Beer:* prices vary according to type and strength, but a half-litre can of lager is approximately £1.50.
- *Cinema ticket:* £5–£10.
- *Theatre ticket:* £10–£30.
- *Concert ticket:* £5–£30.
- *Swimming pool:* £2.50.
- *Tennis/squash court:* £3 per hour.
- *Daily fares:* these will vary according to the distance to be travelled.

6.4 Managing your money

🛈 Dealing in a different currency can be confusing and if you do meet problems, it is important to try to sort them out quickly rather than finding yourself in debt or falling behind with your rent. Once your have opened a bank account, you will be able to use the services of the bank's financial advisers to help you decide how best to manage your money. They can help you organize a budget account to pay regular bills or help you to deal with any periods when you might need an overdraft facility. If you have a financial sponsor, make sure you know exactly the terms and conditions of their support; when money will be made available to you and how much. If you find you are building up debts on credit cards or with rent arrears, debt counselling may be available at your institution or at a local Citizens Advice Bureau. As a general rule, seek help earlier rather than later.

Problems may arise, for example, if there is a sudden change in the political situation in your country, if there are unforeseen delays in the transfer of your money, or perhaps because you find your personal circumstances such as accommodation or marital status have changed. In these situations you must not be tempted to try to find paid employment without the necessary permission and you should not enter into any agreements to borrow money. In the first place, see the student counsellor at your place of study. They will be able to tell you what to do about paying your tuition fees. They will also be able to tell you if there are any college funds or charitable trusts that might be able to help you through a crisis.

Your Embassy or High Commission should offer you advice if the problems stem from political situations or changes in foreign exchange.

6.5   Banking services

Bank accounts
All the main banks in Britain offer special facilities for full-time students and, provided you always keep money in your account and do not overdraw, they do not make charges for students.

Glossary of terms

Cashpoint card
When you open an account with a bank or building society you will normally be offered a cashpoint card which enables you to access your account twenty-four hours a day by using an automated till machine (ATM). These are built into the wall outside the bank and can also be found in a variety of other places such as outside supermarkets, petrol stations and in large shopping centres.

Current account
Bank account for depositing and withdrawing money on which normally no interest is received.

Deposit account
A savings account where money deposited can earn interest. You may have to give notice if you wish to withdraw money and you cannot issue cheques on it.

To deposit
To put money into an account.

Interest
Extra money paid on money you have invested or extra money you pay on money you have borrowed by loans or overdraft.

To overdraw/ *overdraft*	If you overdraw your account, it means you have spent more money than you deposited. When you do this you pay interest and bank charges to the bank. An overdraft is an amount of money agreed between you and the bank by which you may overspend. However, you will still pay interest and bank charges.
PIN	Once you have received your cashpoint card you will be sent a personal identification number (PIN). You should learn this number as you will need to key it into the machine each time you use your card. Once you are sure that you know the number, destroy the slip which had the number written on it and do not write the number down anywhere else. If anyone else gets hold of your card and knows your PIN they will be able to access your account and withdraw money from it.
To withdraw	When you withdraw money you take it from your account by writing a cheque or using a cash card. A cash card allows you to withdraw an agreed amount each week from your account from cash-dispensing machines situated outside banks.

The most useful account to arrange in the first instance is a current account. You can pay in money in cash or by cheque or by banker's draft. Cheques and banker's drafts must be made out to the name of the account holder. In turn you can issue cheques and withdraw cash yourself. You can withdraw cash by writing a cheque payable in your own name or to 'cash'. Eventually, you will be issued with a cash card which allows you to withdraw money from automatic cashpoints situated outside banks and to pay for goods in larger stores and supermarkets.

You can also use cheques to pay for goods and services, although you will need to produce a cheque guarantee card to show that the bank will honour your cheques up to a stated amount. Usually the cheque guarantee card and the cash card are combined. With banking becoming organized more and more on an international basis, you may also find that you can use the cash card you have in your own country to draw money from that account while you are in Britain. Cards carrying signs such as Cirrus or Maestro may have this facility. It is a good idea to check the arrangements before you leave to ensure that you bring the right cards with you.

If you find you are paying large amounts of money into your account, you might find it to your advantage to open a deposit account as well.

Building societies

Building societies were formed originally to lend money for people to buy a house. However, they also offer a range of financial services including banking. You may find that, unlike a main bank, a building society will offer you interest on a current account. If possible, you should visit all the main banks and building societies near your place of study to see which can offer you the best service.

The Post Office

The Post Office also offers a banking service called National Giro as well as a National Savings Bank for money held on deposit to earn interest. In general these accounts are probably not as flexible for international transactions as the services offered by banks and building societies, but you may wish to consider such accounts as an addition to your main account. The National Giro, for example, can be used to pay bills for such services as telephone, water, electricity and gas. However, you can pay these bills by cash or cheque at post offices even without such an account.

Your bank or other account can be used to pay your regular bills such as electricity, gas, telephone by direct debit or by standing order, on a monthly basis. It is important, however, to monitor your account and ensure that you do not go overdrawn. If you do overdraw your account, heavy charges will be imposed and the bank may refuse to honour your cheques. If there are foreseeable problems of cash flow – perhaps you have heavy bills at a time when money is on its way to you but is not yet in your account – then arrange to talk to the bank's representative about your situation. The bank may agree a sum by which you can overdraw your account, but you will still have to pay interest on the money you borrow.

Some short-stay students may have trouble in obtaining full banking services. Nevertheless, it is certainly important to make secure arrangements for your cash. Never carry large sums of money with you or leave a lot of cash in your lodgings.

6.6   Insurance

There are three types of insurance that you should consider once you are in Britain. These are:

- personal property insurance – which covers your possessions against damage or theft;
- motor insurance – a legal requirement for anyone driving a car or motor cycle in Britain;
- medical insurance – covers all medical bills if you are not entitled to NHS services (see Chapter 7).

In all cases, there are many different types of insurance policy available and it is advisable to look around for one which suits your requirements and which you can afford. Before taking out a particular policy, ask yourself the following questions:

- What will be paid out to me when I make a claim? Some personal property insurance policies, for example, only pay you the second-hand value of your lost possession. The more expensive 'new-for-old' policies will pay you the full cost of replacing the item.
- Are there any conditions attached to the policy? Some medical insurance policies will not cover you for pre-existing medical conditions. Some personal property policies may not cover your possessions if they are taken away from the place where they are normally kept (for example, if you take your CD player to a friend's house).
- Are there any exceptions to the policy? For example, a medical insurance policy may not cover you if you play a 'dangerous' sport (find out how they define dangerous sport).

ℹ You will find a wide range of insurance companies listed in your local telephone directory, or your bank or building society may be able to offer you one. Many insurance companies offer special policies for students. One which offers a special policy to students from overseas is Endsleigh Insurance (see address list at end of this

chapter). If you have a complaint about an insurer, or wish to check
the status of an insurance company, you can contact the Association
of British Insurers (see address list at end of this chapter).

6.7   Driving and owning a car or motor cycle

In Britain, anyone wanting to drive a car or motor cycle must have a
valid licence and must be at least seventeen years old (or sixteen
years old if you wish to drive a moped). During your first year in
Britain, you may use your own overseas driving licence or an International Driving Permit. If you are here for more than one year,
unless you come from one of the countries listed below, you will have
to apply for a British provisional licence (details from your local post
office) and retake a driving test. If you come from one of the following
countries, you may exchange your overseas licence for a British
licence: Australia, Austria, Barbados, Belgium, British Virgin
Islands, Republic of Cyprus, Denmark, Finland, France, Germany,
Greece, Hong Kong, Ireland, Italy, Japan, Kenya, Luxembourg,
Netherlands, New Zealand, Norway, Portugal, Singapore, Spain,
Sweden, Switzerland, Zimbabwe.

Some other points of UK driving law
- Motorists must drive on the left-hand side of the road and
  overtake on the right.
- Riders of motor cycles or mopeds must wear a crash-helmet.
- Seat belts must be fitted and worn by driver and passengers in the
  front seats. If seat belts are fitted in the rear seats, these must
  also be worn.
- Do not drive any motor vehicle if you have been drinking alcohol.
- Drivers of all vehicles must observe speed limits. These are
  displayed in signs along the roadside but are usually 30 or
  sometimes 40mph (miles per hour) in towns and built-up areas,
  70mph on motorways and 60mph on all other roads.

Buying/owning a car
If you own a car in Britain it must be registered in your name, taxed,
insured and, if it is over three years old, have a valid MOT certificate.

Registration: when you buy a new or second-hand car you should be
given the car's registration document. You must immediately

register or re-register the car in your name by completing the
document and sending it to the address supplied.

💷 *Tax:* all car owners must pay road tax. This is currently £130 for one
year. Tax can be paid at any main Post Office. On receipt of the fee,
you will be supplied with a tax disc which must be displayed at all
times in your car windscreen.

Insurance: the cost of a car insurance policy will vary according to
your age, how long you have been driving, where you are living, the
age and value of your car and the type of car you have. You can also
choose between three different types of insurance policy:
comprehensive (the fullest cover but also the most expensive); third
party, fire and theft; or third party only (the minimum possible cover
and the least expensive).

MOT: the MOT test is the Ministry of Transport roadworthiness test
and must be taken by cars over three years old. The MOT test is
available at most garages, but make sure that they are an approved
MOT centre (they will display a sign which says this).

6.8   The legal system

If you find yourself involved in legal disputes of any kind, whether of
a civil or a criminal nature, there are a number of agencies you can
contact for help. Your college students' union or welfare officer/
counsellor will either be able to help you directly or advise you
where to go for help. If you do not wish to bring your problem to the
attention of your place of study, then the Citizens Advice Bureau in
your area (see local telephone directory for address) is a good source
of expert advice. They will be able to recommend a solicitor if
necessary and tell you if there is a local law centre providing free
legal advice. They will also be able to tell you whether you are able to
claim legal aid to help pay for any court and legal fees.

In trouble with the law
If you find yourself in trouble with the police it is very important
that you seek professional advice from either:

● your college or university welfare officer;

- the students' union at your college or university;
- your local Citizens Advice Bureau;
- a local law centre.

If you are convicted (found guilty) of an offence this could have serious implications for you as an international student. A record of what has happened will be kept in your Home Office file and this could affect future applications for an extension of your leave to remain in the UK. If you are convicted of a very serious offence then you may be deported.

Arrests

The police have the power to stop and search anyone who appears to be behaving in a suspicious manner. If you are arrested:

- Try not to be aggressive.
- Do not try to bribe the police officer.
- Do not refuse to give your name and address.
- Do not sign any statement until you have received advice from a solicitor. (There will always be a solicitor on duty at the police station.)
- You will be entitled to make one telephone call. If you use this call to phone a friend, make sure that they contact someone from your college or from the students' union to get advice about what you should do next.
- If you are arrested by plain-clothes police officers, ask to see some form of identification.

It is against the law in Britain to:

- Possess offensive weapons – for example, knives (including flick-knives) and guns. Even women are not allowed to carry chemical sprays or other deterrents for personal protection against possible assault.
- Possess or supply hard or soft drugs.
- Steal goods from shops.
- Damage public or private property – any form of vandalism is an offence. As well as having to pay a fine, you will also be required to pay for any damage you have caused.
- Disturb the peace – this is called disorderly conduct and you can, believe it or not, be arrested for being excessively noisy or rowdy.

6.9   Sources of information

Addresses of organizations mentioned in this chapter
Association of British Insurers, 51 Gresham Street, London EC2V 7HQ, Tel: (0)171-600 3333, Fax: (0)171-696 8999.

Endsleigh Insurance, Cranfield House, 97–107 Southampton Row, London WC1B 4AG, Tel: (0)171-436 4451, Fax: (0)171-637 3132.

Further reading
Awards for First Degree Study at Commonwealth Universities,
The Association of Commonwealth Universities, biennial.

Awards for Postgraduate Study at Commonwealth Universities,
The Association of Commonwealth Universities, biennial.

British Council Information Sheets: *Sources of financial assistance for overseas students; Tuition fees and the cost of living.*
The Directory of Grant-making Trusts, Charities Aid Foundation, annual.

The Grants Register, Macmillan, annual.

UKCOSA sheets: *Course fees and grants; European Community students; Financial help; Scholarships for international students* (available from your local British Council office).

7   Health

In this chapter we advise you about the system for health care in Britain.

Britain has a subsidized health service which is called the NHS (National Health Service). The NHS provides free and subsidized treatment for people who are resident in Britain. As an international student you may also be entitled to NHS treatment if you are in any one of the following categories:

- you are enrolled on a course lasting for more than six months;
- you are a national or resident of an EEA country;
- you are from a country which has a reciprocal health agreement with Britain (Anguilla, Australia, Barbados, British Virgin Islands, Bulgaria, Channel Islands, Croatia, Czech and Slovak Republics, Falkland Islands, Gibraltar, Hong Kong, Hungary, Isle of Man, Malta, Montserrat, New Zealand, Poland, Romania, Russia and the former Soviet Union States (except Latvia, Lithuania and Estonia), the former Yugoslavia).

If you are not entitled to NHS treatment then you will have to see doctors and dentists as a 'charged NHS patient' and pay the full cost of any treatment given. As this can be very expensive, you are advised to take out a medical insurance policy.

7.1   Emergencies

Accident and emergency services are free for everyone in the first instance, although if you are admitted to hospital for any treatment as a result of an accident, and you are not covered by the NHS, then you will have to pay for this treatment.

In an emergency you should either phone for an ambulance (telephone 999) or get someone to take you to the casualty (accident and emergency) department of the nearest hospital.

7.2   Registering with a doctor

If you are eligible for NHS treatment you are also entitled to register with a local doctor. You should do this as soon as possible after you arrive in Britain and not wait until you are ill. If your college or university has a health centre, you may be able to register with a doctor there, or they will be able to recommend a local doctor. Otherwise, you can obtain a list of local doctors from the Family Health Services Agency (FHSA) in your area (the address will be in your local telephone directory, under the relevant area).

When you have registered with a doctor you will eventually receive a medical card stating your NHS number. You should take this card with you whenever you go to see your doctor.

When you go to your doctor for the first time, be sure to find out the times when the surgery is open. Also ask whether the surgery operates an appointment-only system. There should also be an emergency telephone number which you can call if you need to see a doctor outside the normal surgery opening hours.

If the doctor prescribes any medicines, he or she will give you a prescription which you have to take to a chemist. You will then be charged for each item on your prescription. The fee is currently £5.25 per item.

7.3   Dentists

In Britain, everyone has to pay something towards the cost of their dental treatment, even regular check-ups. However, if you are eligible for NHS treatment, you can also receive dental treatment at a reduced rate. You should register with a local dentist as soon as possible. Before you register, make sure that the particular dentist takes NHS patients, as some dentists only take on private patients who pay for the full cost of their treatment. You always need to have an appointment to see a dentist but make sure that you let them know if you cannot attend, otherwise you will be charged a cancellation fee.

7.4   Opticians

All patients have to pay for eye tests (around £17), lenses and frames
for spectacles. Prices for these vary considerably from place to place
so have a look around before buying anything. You will probably find
that glasses are more expensive in Britain than in your home
country, so if you do wear glasses, it might be a good idea to bring a
spare pair with you.

7.5   Minor ailments

If you find you are worried by unusual symptoms, try to remember
that travel to a new country with a different climate and diet can
often cause minor health upsets. You may find yourself subject to
coughs, colds and influenza for the first time. If you have never

*'It is also important to maintain a healthy eating style ... also, try
to take a certain amount of exercise'*

experienced such minor illnesses, the symptoms can seem quite worrying. Usually such health matters are easily treated. Make an appointment to see your doctor and explain any differences in your lifestyle that might help to explain why you are vulnerable to minor ailments.

It is also important to maintain a healthy eating style, even though the new foods may not be ones you particularly enjoy. If you are eating a lot of fast foods, take-away meals or quick snacks (burgers, crisps, etc.) try to supplement your diet with plenty of fresh fruit and vegetables.

Also try to take a certain amount of exercise. If you dislike sport, go for a few long walks or even take exercise classes!

7.6   Women's health

Women students may wish to register with a female doctor and they have the right to do this. Contraception and advice on birth control are available through your doctor but there are also NHS family planning clinics in each area. These provide free services to women students provided they are normally entitled to free NHS treatment.

If you become pregnant during your stay, then help and advice is available from the welfare officer or student counsellor at your place of study. They will be able to refer you to appropriate professionals if necessary. Alternatively your doctor or the local family planning clinic can advise you of your rights and options. Please note, however, that no insurance cover is available for the cost of pregnancy or the delivery of a baby for students here for less than six months or for the wife of a student, even if she is normally eligible for treatment. The British Pregnancy Advisory Service has branches in major cities throughout Britain. Your local Citizens Advice Bureau can tell you where the nearest office is, or you can contact the head office (address at the end of this chapter).

If you have other worries about your health, advice and check-ups are available from Well Woman Clinics in many areas. Your GP or college will be able to tell where the nearest clinic is.

If you have been subject to any form of physical harassment or
sexual assault then it is vital to seek help and advice immediately
ⓘ Most large towns and cities have a Rape Crisis Centre. You will be
able to find their number in the local telephone directory.

7.7   Sexually transmitted diseases

You may find that attitudes to sex in Britain are different from those
in your own country. Sexual relationships here are entirely a matter
of personal choice. With sexual freedom, however, there are additional risks of catching sexually transmitted diseases which can
range from those treated easily with antibiotics to HIV/Aids, which
is still incurable and potentially life-threatening. If you think you
have been in danger of catching such an illness you should contact
your doctor, who will treat your case in confidence. You may also
enquire if there is a unit specializing in such illnesses at the local
hospital. If you are worried about Aids there are telephone helplines
you can ring for free and confidential advice. The national helpline
ⓘ is 0800 567 123. The Aids telephone helpline also has foreign
language services:

- Cantonese: Tuesdays 6–10 p.m. (0800 282446)
- Arabic: Wednesdays 6–10 p.m. (0800 282477)
- Hindi, Punjabi, Gujarati, Bengali and Urdu: Wednesday 6–10 p.m.
  (0800 282445)

7.8   Drugs and alcohol

In Britain drugs may be used legally only under medical supervision.
For this reason anyone buying drugs from other sources for personal
use may feel afraid of seeking help when they feel their drug use is
becoming a problem. If you need help then you can telephone
ⓘ Turning Point (0171-702 2300) for confidential advice. It is not illegal
for people over eighteen to buy and consume alcoholic drinks but if
you find that you are drinking too much you could seek help from
your student counsellor or your doctor. You can also telephone your
local branch of Alcoholics Anonymous by looking for the number in
the telephone directory.

7.9　Services for disabled people

Public buildings in Britain have a legal obligation to be accessible to disabled people. In theory, therefore, you should be able to go to museums, theatres, restaurants – all places you may wish to visit – without difficulty. In practice, many older buildings still cause problems for disabled people, so it is sensible to check in advance of a visit that you will be able to get in.

Public transport remains a problem, especially for wheelchair users. Trains have facilities for wheelchair users, but buses generally do not. The London Underground is largely inaccessible to wheelchair uses because of the escalators. This means that you have to check the availability of transport before you undertake any trip. Some taxis are specially converted to take wheelchairs, but check before you order one.

Disabled car-users can apply for a badge entitling them to free parking. There are also tour operators and organizations arranging trips and holidays with access for disabled people. For information about these services, contact the Royal Association for Disability and Rehabilitation or SKILL (addresses at the end of this chapter).

7.10　Health care checklist

- ✓ Check whether you are entitled to health care under the NHS.
- ✓ Arrange any necessary or additional insurance.
- ✓ Register with a doctor as soon as you can.
- ✓ Take care to eat a properly balanced diet and to take regular exercise at your institution.
- ✓ If you have health concerns discuss them with your doctor, your college welfare officer or student counsellor so that you can be advised of the best course of action.

7.11　Sources of information

Addresses of organizations mentioned in this chapter
The British Pregnancy Advisory Service (BPAS), Austey Manor, Wootton Wawen, Solihull, West Midlands BN95 6BX, Tel: (01564) 793225, Fax: (01564) 794935.

Royal Association for Disability and Rehabilitation (RADAR), 250 City Road, London EC1V 8AF, Tel: (0)171-250 3222.

SKILL (National Bureau for Students with Disabilities), 336 Brixton Road, London SW9 7AA, Tel: (0)171-274 0565.

National Association of Citizens Advice Bureaux, Myddleton House, 115–123 Pentonville Road, London N1 9LZ, Tel: (0)171-833 2181.

Further reading
UKCOSA sheets: *Keeping healthy; Welfare benefits and international students* (available from your local British Council office).

8 Student life – study

In this chapter we look at studying patterns and how you can adapt to them.

8.1 Studying

The stresses of living and working in a new environment can mean that you find studying harder than you had imagined. You may feel concerned about your progress, you may worry that you are behind the other students in your group, you may start to worry about failing examinations. These fears are entirely natural but there are a number of ways to keep control of your studying patterns so that you do not become anxious and ineffective.

You can ask for regular meetings with your tutor to review your progress and discuss any problems. If you think you are having problems because of language difficulties, your tutor will be able to advise you how to deal with this. There may, for example, be a language centre at your college or university with self-access language-learning materials. There may be a programme of English classes designed specifically for international students.

You can try forming a mutual support group with others of your nationality or with other overseas students to discuss common problems and share solutions. This could be particularly helpful if you find the teaching methods in the UK very different from those you have experienced before. Another type of support group could come from within your subject area. Students on similar courses can also meet to discuss their progress, their reactions to the courses, to swap ideas and give each other support.

Never let your difficulties with studying overwhelm you. The student counsellor at your place of study as well as the academic staff in your department will be able to offer real support and constructive advice. Often, your problems can be caused by setting yourself unrealistic targets. Talking to the academic staff and the counsellor will help you put the problems into perspective.

8.2   Teaching styles

You may well come from a country where the education system is
very different from the British system and you may also find teaching
and learning methods that you are unfamiliar with. In fact, even
British students are surprised by the differences between teaching
methods and attitudes in school and those found in further and
higher education.

Some aspects of further and higher education which you may be
unused to:

- You will not be required to attend classes all the time and will
  have much more time to study on your own. This means that you
  will have to organize your private study time.
- Your teacher/tutors/lecturers will not always provide you with
  answers. They will provide you with the means to find the
  answers yourself.
- You will not always be dealing with facts and right or wrong
  answers. You will also be dealing with opinions – and your own
  opinions will be as valid as anyone else's.
- Classroom teaching may be much more informal than you are
  used to. You will be much more actively involved, encouraged to
  ask questions, join in discussions, even argue with your tutors.

Lectures

Lectures are the most formal teaching situation, in which the
lecturer addresses a large group of students. Unless you are copying
down mathematical or scientific formulae, you do not have to try to
write down everything the lecturer says. Make notes of the main
ideas and any references you should follow up. If possible do some
preparatory reading before the lecture so that you know what it is
going to be about – and maybe you will be able to form some opinions
of your own. After the lecture it is a good idea to look at your notes
and arrange them and add to them any thoughts of your own so that
they will be useful reference points later on.

You will probably find that no one checks to see if you have attended
lectures, so you have to discipline yourself to go to them. Do not take
the attitude that it doesn't matter if you miss lectures, just because
no one checks. The only person who will suffer is you.

If you must miss a lecture, make sure that you borrow someone's notes so that you don't miss anything important.

Seminars and tutorials

Seminars are small discussion groups where a number of students join their lecturer to discuss and exchange ideas on a particular topic. Do not be afraid to join in discussions because you are not sure whether your English is good enough. The other students will want to hear your ideas and opinions and do not want to criticize your English grammar. Sometimes, one or more of you will be asked to prepare a paper in advance which you will then have to present to the rest of the group. The other students will then be invited to discuss and criticize your paper. This will probably be a new experience for everyone and so you will all be equally nervous at first.

Tutorials are held between a lecturer (tutor) and one student or a small group of three or four students. They are the opportunity for you to discuss your own work or a particular topic in greater depth. Some colleges assign students a 'personal tutor' whose responsibility it is to help the students with any difficulties they are having with their work.

8.3   Organizing your time

When you have worked out your timetable of lectures, seminars and tutorials, you may be surprised to find that you have quite a lot of free time. This is the time that you must organize and divide between study time and free time. If you do not organize your time systematically then you will spend all of your time on things that you really enjoy and no time on the things which you find most difficult. Time which isn't organized can disappear very quickly and you may find that you are always having to stay up late working on an essay due in the following day when you knew you had to write it several weeks before. It is also important to remember that not all of this free time is meant for studying and you should allocate some time to hobbies, sports, seeing friends or simply relaxing and preparing yourself mentally and physically in whatever way suits you best.

It is a good idea to make weekly or even monthly plans which set out your study targets for the week or month ahead, or even make a timetable for your free time, in the same way that you would make and follow a timetable for your classes. Establishing routines, and being in control of your time, means that your time will be used more effectively.

8.4   Sources of information

Further reading
D. Rowntree, *Learn How to Study: a guide for students of all ages*, Warner, 1991, £6.99.

9   Student life – leisure

In this chapter we examine the opportunities you will have to enjoy your free time. If you plan to spend several months or even years in Britain, you will want to take advantage of the wide range of cultural, social and leisure activities available, as well as opportunities for travel within and outside Britain.

9.1   Social life at your university or college

During the first week of a new term or semester, and after any orientation programme which has been arranged specifically for international students, there will be a programme of social events for new students which is usually referred to as the freshers' fair or freshers' week. Freshers' week provides you with the opportunity to find out what leisure and social facilities are available at the institution and it is also a good time to start meeting people and making friends. Some of the activities which you might expect to find during freshers' week are:

- receptions (light refreshments) hosted by specific departments or by the Vice-Chancellor, for example;
- discos and dances;
- 'intro fairs', where you are invited to join a variety of clubs and societies run by the students' union.

The students' union

The National Union of Students (NUS) is a national body representing the interests of all students in the UK. All universities and most of the larger colleges have a students' union of which you are automatically a member. After the first week of term, you will probably find that most of the entertainment programmes and social activities available at your university or college are arranged by the students' union. You will often find that there will be a union building somewhere on the campus which has restaurants, bars, shop and a variety of other facilities, all run by the students' union.

'"Freshers' Week" allows you to find out what leisure and social facilities are available'

The students' union also provides other services to its members such as a welfare and advice service, information about student travel, sport and leisure facilities.

9.2   Social life outside the institution

You may, of course, wish to extend your social life beyond your place of study. Leisure facilities and activities will vary depending on which part of Britain you are in. For example, you may be living in a large city with hundreds of theatres, cinemas, museums, and so on, or you may be in a small town which has just one cinema. The best places to find out about what is available in your town or city are:

● local newspapers;
● entertainment listings magazines (such as *Time Out* in London and *City Life* in Manchester);
● local libraries;
● your students' union.

If you want to meet British people you will probably need to involve yourself in some sort of activity such as evening classes, where you might learn more about a particular interest or hobby, or by joining a sports club or an amateur dramatic society or choir. It is quite difficult to meet people casually in bars and cafés, especially in larger cities, as people do not tend to talk to anyone they don't know, but by joining them in a particular activity, you will be able to get to know them in a more natural environment. You might also consider joining a local church or other religious group where you can meet people who practise the same religion as you.

Another way to get to know British people is to go and stay with them as guests in their homes. There are two organizations in Britain which arrange to put you in touch with British families who would like to have a visitor from overseas as a guest for a weekend or during the vacation, particularly at Christmas. You can find their addresses at the end of this chapter.

9.3   Local amenities

Public libraries

No doubt your college or university will have a library of its own but you might also wish to join your local public library. As well as being places where you can read and study in peace, borrow books and often videos and music cassettes as well, they are also useful centres of local information. In a public library you will be able to find information on local services, including lists of local doctors, and social events taking place locally. Joining a library is free of charge – all you need to do is complete a form and provide proof of your address.

Shopping

Shopping facilities in Britain are extensive and diverse. Most medium-sized or large towns have street markets, which are a source of fresh foods and cheaper household goods, clothing and miscellaneous items. Over recent years shopping centres, malls and hypermarkets have been built outside towns incorporating food stores, furniture shops, do-it-yourself shops and most other goods. Such centres are usually open seven days a week. Chain-store supermarkets such as Tesco, Sainsbury, Safeway, Waitrose, Morrisons, and Asda usually offer a comprehensive range of foodstuffs, including many international items. These shops can offer competitive pricing, particularly if you look for the stores' own brands of goods. If you go to these shops shortly before their closing times, you can often buy fresh foods at reduced prices because the shop must sell them on that day.

Town-centre high streets have a range of individual and chain shops for everyday needs. Chains that you will find in almost every town are:

W.H. Smith	*newsagents and bookseller*
Boots	*chemists*
Woolworths	*general*
Marks & Spencer	*general*
British Home Stores (BHS)	*general*
Littlewoods	*general*
Dillons	*books*
Waterstones	*books*

In addition there are chains of clothes shops and health-food shops.

Restrictions on shop opening times have been relaxed considerably but you may still find that they close earlier than in your own country. Most large stores do not close for lunch but smaller shops may. In general shop opening times are from 9.00 a.m. to 5.30 p.m. Monday to Saturday, with some opening on Sundays. Some large stores have 'late opening' on one or more days per week. Small local shops also often stay open late. Chemists' shops work to a local rota system so that there is normally one open most of the time in each area for emergency supplies.

At certain times of the year shops hold clearance sales and reduce the prices of their goods. The main sales occur in January and late summer. Bar codes are replacing price tags on the goods in shops, especially in supermarkets, so make sure you check the price (usually marked on the shelf or near the items) before you buy anything. Although most foods and books and newspapers do not carry VAT (value added tax), most other items include VAT at 17.5 per cent of the price. Larger and more expensive items, such as cars, may be displayed with a price excluding VAT.

Clothing

If you are coming to Britain from a country with a very different climate, you may wish to buy some items of clothing for the wet, cold and windy times in this country. Even if you intend to continue wearing your national dress, you will find that you need a warm overcoat or a raincoat in the winter. Fortunately, there are inexpensive chain stores (such as Marks and Spencer, C & A, British

Home Stores, Littlewoods) in nearly every town's high street. In these stores you can find competitively priced clothing to suit every season. Charity shops in town centres are good sources of second-hand clothing in good condition. The main ones are Oxfam, Sue Ryder and Cancer Research. Local village halls and church halls also have regular jumble sales to raise money. The sales are of goods that householders wish to dispose of but cannot sell. Inevitably much 'jumble' is not very interesting, but these sales can be another source of second-hand clothing. The car-parks of supermarkets, hospitals and schools sometimes hold car-boot sales where individuals can bring goods they wish to sell and deal directly with customers. These too can be a source of second-hand clothing. If you buy electrical or mechanical items from jumble sales or car-boot sales, check that the items actually work before you buy, as there are no guarantees or refunds for goods bought in this way. (See Chapter 6, Section 6.3 for a rough guide to clothes prices.)

Clothing sizes

Clothes and shoes in Britain are given different sizes from those in Europe and the USA. However, most labels will contain information stating metric and US sizes as well. If in doubt about the size of an item, ask to try it on before you buy it or ask the shop assistant to measure you for the appropriate British size.

Consumer rights

Under British law consumers have the right to return faulty goods to the shop where they were bought within one year of purchase and receive either a replacement or a refund. Proof of purchase will probably be required and this protection does not extend to goods you have accidentally damaged yourself. If you have a problem over goods you have bought and feel you have not been justly recompensed by the shop, you can go to the local Office of Fair Trading to make a complaint. The address will be available at your local library or from the telephone directory.

Many goods are made to government-controlled standards and bear a British Standards Institute (BSI) label.

Eating out

The British have acquired a taste for food from many different cultures and the first question is often: 'What kind of food do you feel

like: Indian? Chinese? Italian? Thai? Vietnamese? vegetarian?' One
reason for the popularity of these types of restaurant is that they are
often much cheaper than the more traditional British ones, which
serve a mixture of British and French cooking.

In the larger cities you will find almost every nationality represented
by way of restaurants serving specialist or 'national' food. You would
probably be wise, initially, to get someone to recommend a few places
to suit your palate and your pocket (i.e. within your price range).
People are often only too pleased to share new restaurant 'finds' with
friends and acquaintances.

Take-away food

Restaurants often have a take-away service so you can buy cooked
food and take it to eat elsewhere. The most common are the
American 'fast-food' hamburger restaurants, along with Indian,
Chinese and Italian pizza take-aways. Many pizza take-aways provide
delivery services so you don't even have to go out to the restaurant –
you just phone through your order and pay when the pizza is brought
to your door. The original British take-away food is fried fish and
chips (potatoes/french fries). There are thousands of fish and chip
shops nationwide.

Self-service

Another cheap way to eat out is to go to a self-service café where
you can serve yourself from a counter and pay for your food before
eating it. Many self-service restaurants now offer a good range of

salads and hot meals but some offer mainly fried food of the sausage, egg and chip variety. Motorway service stations usually offer a self-service restaurant amongst their facilities and, although they once had a poor reputation for the sort of food they offered and prices they charged for it, consumer pressure groups have forced a change. Nowadays you will find a reasonable variety of hot and cold foods available.

Restaurants

Restaurants with waiter service are usually more expensive than the places mentioned but beyond that it is impossible to generalize. Most restaurants display a menu outside the premises so you can see the type of food served and the range of prices. In restaurants there may be a cover charge of so much per head, and you will be expected to pay a 'service charge', or tip of at least ten per cent. Bear in mind, too, that drinks will usually cost more in a restaurant than in a shop or pub but most restaurants are licensed to serve alcohol whereas cheaper places are often not. Two things to check: usually menu prices include VAT, but make sure. Also check when the bill comes that a service charge has not already been added to it, otherwise you could end up paying it twice.

There are various guides to the restaurants of Britain which describe the menus, the quality and the prices of meals available. One such is the *Good Food Guide* (Hodder) which lists about 1,500 restaurants and is revised every year. Check to see what information you can find at your place of study as well. Often students' unions publish guides to local restaurants.

Alcohol

Anyone may drink alcohol in Britain but you must be over eighteen to buy it or drink it on licensed premises. Places that sell alcohol have to be licensed and are governed by the licensing laws as to when they can open. English public houses or 'pubs' are allowed to open between 11.00 a.m. and 11.00 p.m. except on Sundays, when the hours are 12.00 p.m. to 3.00 p.m. and 7.00 p.m. to 10.30 p.m. However, individual landlords may choose their own hours within these limits and while pubs may be open during all available hours in cities, in rural areas more restricted times may be chosen. Scotland, Wales and Northern Ireland have their own but similar licensing laws and the opening and closing times vary slightly as a result. Some counties in Wales and some of the Scottish islands are 'dry' on Sunday, i.e. it is illegal to buy or sell alcohol on Sundays.

Pubs and wine bars

Pubs are an important part of British social life, where people meet and talk. Beer is traditionally the national drink. You may find it much heavier than beer at home – if you want a lighter beer, ask for lager. Pubs often serve food, particularly at lunchtime, which is usually cheap and tasty. A 'free house' is a pub which sells the beer of several different breweries; many pubs are owned by breweries and sell, mainly, their beer. In restaurants with a table licence, that is, a licence to sell alcohol only with food, the licensing hours are longer and children of all ages can be admitted. Clubs also generally have special extended licences. Bars inside restaurants, hotels or other buildings, however, are governed by the same rules as pubs. Off-licences are special shops licensed to sell alcohol to be drunk off the premises. Many stick to pub hours but they can vary. Most supermarkets also have an off-licence section.

Drinking alcohol is not frowned upon in Britain, though getting very drunk is. Drunkenness, particularly if linked with driving, can get you arrested. Most people enjoy a drink either for its own sake or for social reasons and people will often meet in a pub or bar for a drink at lunchtime or perhaps in the early evening in between work and going home. People will also usually offer you a drink when you visit them at home or go to a party. In all these cases it is possible to ask for a non-alcoholic drink – never feel you have to have an alcoholic drink if you don't want to . If you feel strongly about going to places selling alcohol, make this clear to your British friends. There are usually alternative places where you can meet, such as cafés. One alternative to the pub is the wine bar, where people generally drink wine or fruit juice rather than beer or spirits, and it has less of the atmosphere of heavy drinking than many pubs.

Telephones

Public telephones in Britain are now nearly always steel and glass kiosks bearing the British Telecom (BT) logo. They are either coin-operated or card-operated. If they are card-operated you need to obtain a BT phonecard from the nearest newsagent, post office or supermarket. These cards entitle you to a specific number of units and you can buy cards to the value of £2, £5, £10 and £20. Most call boxes have a display panel to tell you where and how to insert your BT phonecard, when to dial and when to hang up. Before you dial you should listen for a continuous high-pitched hum. The engaged tone is a repeated single note and, when your money or card is running out, you hear rapid pips. If a number is unavailable you hear a steady tone.

Telephone numbers
Telephone numbers are always written in groups of numbers, for example:

- (0171)-482 1456
- (0181)-887 5357
- (0161)-592 4836

The numbers in brackets are the codes you need to dial if you are outside that particular area. For example, 0161 is the code for Manchester. If you are inside the Manchester area, you would not need to dial 0161, just the rest of the number. If you are dialling to Britain from overseas you do not dial the first 0 of any number.

ⓘ If you do not know the telephone number for a person or an organization anywhere in Britain, and you do not have a telephone directory, you can call Directory Enquiries on 192. This call will be free from public pay phones but not from private phones. The Yellow Pages telephone directory lists addresses and telephone numbers of local businesses and services.

International calls
ⓘ To make calls overseas you need to dial 00 first, then the country code followed by the number you require. Country codes, as well as national codes, are listed in the front of all telephone directories but if you do not have a directory you can obtain the code by dialling 155 for the international operator. If you don't know the telephone number of the person you wish to call, you can dial 153 for International Directory Enquiries. These days there are very few places in the world which cannot be dialled directly, but if you do need to call one of these, you can make a call through the international operator (155).

Cheap rates

Inland calls are cheapest between 6.00 p.m. and 8.00 a.m. Overseas calls are cheapest between 8.00 p.m. and 8.00 a.m. There are also reduced rates on Saturday and Sunday.

Summary of useful numbers:

Domestic operator	100
International operator	155
Inland directory enquiries	192
Overseas directory enquiries	153
International dialling code	00
Emergency services	999

Postal service

Post offices are usually open from 9.00 a.m. to 5.30 p.m., Monday to Friday and from 9.00 a.m. to 12.30 p.m. on Saturday. Stamps can also be bought at newsagents and other shops. There are also wall-mounted vending machines selling stamps in books of four or ten. Letter post for the UK has a two-tier system, with first-class mail intended to arrive the next day and second-class mail arriving a day or two later. If you have important documents to send by post, then recorded delivery or registered post systems are safer. Recorded delivery gives the sender proof that the letter has been posted and received. Registered post has additional safeguards including compensation if the item is lost. Cash should never be sent through the post. Use cheques, postal orders or international money orders instead.

The cost of sending an item through the post depends on its weight and where it has to go. Within Britain, a normal letter (under 20g in weight) will cost 25p to send by first-class post or 19p to send by second-class post. To send the same letter overseas would cost between 30p and 60p, depending on exactly where it was being sent. Full details of postal charges can be obtained at any post office.

Other services

Hairdressers range from luxury salons to small-town local shops with prices to match. In bigger towns where hairdressers may be working as trainees or apprentices, free or reduced-cost cutting and styling is often available if you are willing to allow a trainee to cut your hair under supervision.

Launderettes are widely available for washing, drying and, sometimes, ironing your clothes. These contain coin-operated machines where you can do your own laundry or leave it with the attendant to do on your behalf for a service charge.

Dry cleaners will take heavier items of clothing or delicate items and clean them, sometimes on the same day or after a day or two.

Shoe repairers are found in high streets, shopping malls, bus and railway stations and sometimes inside department stores and will usually carry out repairs while you wait.

Television and video-players may be rented (or bought, of course) but remember that each household requires a television licence (£86.50 per annum).

9.4 Travel and transport facilities

Britain has an extensive network of trains and buses both for inter-city and local journeys. Internal air travel is also available and, although it is usually expensive, it sometimes has rates competitive with other forms of transport. For very long train journeys, sleepers are sometimes available and cars can be taken on some trains via the Motorail service. Maps of the London Underground and current Intercity routes appear inside the front and back covers of this book

ⓘ If you purchase a Young Person's Railcard or a Student Coach Card you will be entitled to reduced fares on most journeys. Details about these cards can be obtained from your students' union office or from any main railway or coach station.

For rail travel there is a very complex structure for fares, so you should ensure that you have bought the right ticket for your journey:

- *Savers:* return tickets that can be used at weekends, bank holidays and weekdays outside peak travel times.
- *Super Savers:* return tickets with more limitations on travel times than savers.
- *Apex:* inter-city tickets limited in availability which must be bought seven days in advance.

- *Super Apex:* tickets available for some journeys which have to be bought two weeks in advance.
- *Travelcards:* these tickets can cover all forms of transport in London. If you travel to London from another town, the travel card can combine your main journey with travel around the capital.
- *Railcards and Network cards:* these are cards lasting for a year entitling the holder to reductions on rail journeys. Peak-hour travel is excluded.
- *Rover tickets:* these tickets allow you unlimited travel in a specific area, usually for one week.

9.5   Using your own transport

Motoring organizations

If you have decided to buy a car for use in Britain you may find it helpful to join one of the number of organizations which offer breakdown and recovery services as well as insurance and route-planning advice and a range of other information about motoring and motoring laws and regulations. The two best-known are the Automobile Association (AA) and the Royal Automobile Club (RAC) (addresses for these organizations are given at the end of this chapter). However, there are others and it is worth asking advice on special rates for students from the National Union of Students.

Distances

Signposts in Britain give distances between places in miles. To convert miles to kilometres divide by five and multiply by eight (fifty miles is approximately eighty kilometres).

The Highway Code

British traffic regulations are contained in *The Highway Code* which is obtainable from most bookshops. Although most road signs are international, it is advisable to familiarize yourself with this code and if you do have to take a driving test in Britain, you will be asked questions about it as part of the test.

Bicycles

If you wish to use a bicycle while you are in Britain, enquire at your place of study whether there are any familiarization courses you can attend (sometimes run by the local police or the local authority) to help you learn how to ride a bicycle safely while you are here. It is not compulsory to wear a safety helmet on a bicycle, but it is advisable to do so. You must also ensure that your bicycle is properly lit if you ride at night and you are yourself wearing items of reflective clothing at these times. You will also need a good locking device, particularly in university towns where bicycles are the favourite mode of transport for students. You can also arrange to have a special number engraved on your bicycle and registered with the police to help ensure its recovery and identification should it be stolen.

9.6   Sources of information

Addresses of organizations mentioned in this chapter
Automobile Association (AA), Norfolk House, Priestley Road, Hampshire RG24 9NY, Tel: (0) 1256 20123

Royal Automobile Club (RAC), 89 Pall Mall, London SW1Y 5HS, Tel: (0) 171-930 2345.

Experiment in International Living, Otesaga, West Malvern Road, Malvern, Worcester WR14 4EN, Tel: (0) 16845 62577 (arranges short-stay accommodation with host families).

Hosting for Overseas Students (HOST), 3 New Burlington Mews, London W1R 8LU, Tel: (0) 171-494 2468 (arranges family stays free of charge).

The National Union of Students (NUS), Nelson Mandela House, 461 Holloway Road, London N7 6LJ, Tel: (0) 171-272 8900.

Further reading
Fodor's Affordable Great Britain – How to See the Best for Less, Fodor's Travel Publications, 1994, £12.99.

The International Student's A–Z: a Guide to Studying and Living in London, International Students House, 229 Great Portland Street, London W1N 5HD, 1995, free.

The Student Book, Macmillan, annual, £12.99.

The Student Guide, Time Out Publications, annual.

10 Living in Britain

In this chapter we discuss some of the most noticeable characteristics of British life.

10.1 Summary of British culture and politics

Britain consists of three different countries: England, Scotland and Wales. The countries of Britain, together with Northern Ireland, make up what is referred to as the United Kingdom. Although relatively small, the different countries within the UK have their own very different character and identity.

In addition, Britain has a tradition of incorporating migrant populations who have sought political refuge here or who have looked for improved opportunities in work or education. This means that, particularly in larger towns and cities, the population is often diversely multi-cultural.

Britain is a monarchy, with the Queen as the official head of government, but the laws of the land are in fact made by Parliament. There is a two-tier system of government: the House of Commons, which consists of 650 members elected by the people of the UK; and a House of Lords, membership of which is either hereditary or conferred by the Queen.

The House of Commons initiates laws and the House of Lords is there to help revise and amend them before they are adopted.

Each member of the House of Commons belongs to a political party. The main political parties are the Conservative Party (currently in government), the Labour Party and the Liberal Democratic Party. There are many smaller parties and several nationalist parties and these often have a few representatives in Parliament.

After a general election, which normally takes place every five years, the political party which wins the most seats in the House of Commons (has the largest number of representatives) forms the government. The leader of that party becomes the Prime Minister.

British citizens can vote at the age of eighteen.

At local level some administration is handled by elected local authorities. It is this system that makes it possible for even quite large towns to have local administrations run by a different political party from the one in power at national level.

10.2   Features of British life

British reserve
The British, and in particular the English, have a reputation for keeping their emotions private and for being reserved in their public behaviour. Such generalizations usually have some foundation in truth but clearly cannot be applied to an entire nation of over 56 million people. The Scots, the Welsh and the Northern Irish may also feel that they do not deserve to be included in this view. There are marked regional differences in England as well, with people in the North often appearing more spontaneous and open than the people of London and the South-East. The basic reputation probably stems from some aspects of British life that overseas visitors note as typically British. On public transport, for example, people do not usually talk to other passengers. On meeting, people do not embrace and usually just shake hands only on a first introduction. In theatres, concert halls and cinemas, audiences are quiet during performances and reactions are often restrained. In traffic, drivers reserve use of their horns for alerting others to danger rather than a show of impatience. None of these behaviour traits, however, need be interpreted by visitors as unfriendliness and in general, if a visitor makes the first move to start a conversation, they will find that British people are helpful and considerate. On the other hand, some aspects of British behaviour may seem lacking in reserve to people from other cultures. An example is the informal use of first names among colleagues holding different status at work.

Visiting a British home
Some useful hints:

- People often socialize at home but unless you know someone very well it is not usual to just 'drop in' without at least telephoning first to make sure that it is convenient.

- If you accept an invitation to a meal in someone's home, it is regarded as a definite appointment and it would be considered bad manners not to turn up. If you really do have to cancel an invitation, do let your hosts know as soon as possible, before they start making preparations.
- If there are certain foods that you cannot eat, do let your host know in advance, in order to save embarrassment on the day.
- Whether you are visiting just for a meal or for a longer stay, it is customary to take a small gift for your host – flowers, chocolates or a bottle of wine, for example.
- If you are actually staying with a British family, the main advice is to act thoughtfully at all times. Some examples: be on time for meals; if you need to miss a meal let your host know; keep your room tidy; let your hosts know if you are going to be staying out late so they won't worry about you; offer to help with household chores – your offer will probably be turned down but will still be appreciated.

Mealtimes for the British, except perhaps for younger people, follow quite a fixed pattern. Breakfast may be anything from toast or a bowl of cereal to a full cooked breakfast consisting of eggs, bacon, sausages and tomatoes. The midday meal, which might be referred to as lunch or dinner depending on which part of Britain you are in, is usually a light meal, except on Sundays when people often have a traditional roast (joint of meat). If members of the family are working or studying, lunch is not normally eaten at home. The evening meal is normally the main meal of the day and may be called either dinner or tea. If you are invited to someone's home for 'tea' it is likely that you will be offered food and not simply a cup of tea.

Languages
Even if you have reached a high level of proficiency in English through studying in your own country, do not be surprised or disappointed if you find it difficult to understand spoken English when you arrive. People will speak faster than you expected; they will use many colloquial expressions with which you are unfamiliar, and across the country you will find many different accents and dialects. If you don't understand, simply ask people to repeat the message more slowly. You will find that you gradually get used to English as it is spoken in Britain.

Place-names

Gloucester, Dyfed and Berwick are typical of place-names that
visitors find hard to pronounce. There are many such problems,
indeed one place name in Wales has fifty-two letters. Unfortunately
it is impossible to give rules for the pronunciation of British place-
names. It is advisable to write down the name of the place you have
to visit or need to know about and show this to whoever you are
talking to.

Queuing

In general people do still form queues in shops, banks and at bus
stops. If you do not follow this general rule, you may find that people
become angry as queue-jumping is considered impolite.

Race relations

People in Britain are protected in law against racial discrimination.
There are areas, however, particularly in parts of major cities, in
which racial tension can be a problem. Seek advice from your place
of study if you are worried about this. If you feel you have been
subject to any form of racial discrimination, you should report it to
the local branch of the Commission for Racial Equality. The
telephone number will be in your telephone directory.

Gays/lesbians

Homosexuality is not illegal in Britain, but the age of consent for
men is eighteen as opposed to sixteen for heterosexual men and
women. Attitudes towards gay lifestyles vary from acceptance
through to ignorance, fear and suspicion, even hostility from some
groups. In more sophisticated big cities there are clubs, pubs and
other meeting places for gays and lesbians. If in doubt, discreet
behaviour is advisable. As for anyone who is sexually active,
precautions against infection from HIV/Aids should be taken.

Smoking

It is illegal to sell cigarettes to anyone under the age of sixteen.
Smoking is often banned in public places and fines are imposed
if this rule is broken in such places as railway carriages or
London Underground stations. Restaurants usually provide non-
smoking areas.

Water

It is safe to drink water from the tap in Britain, although there is a fashion for drinking bottled water. Rivers and lakes may, however, be polluted and you should check before using them for swimming and certainly you should never drink from them. Sea bathing is possible on many British beaches, but it is also true that many are polluted. Check locally before you swim in the sea.

Gas supplies

Natural gas is available in most parts of Britain, although not all country areas. If you find yourself in accommodation using gas for cooking and heating, ensure that you use the appliances in accordance with the safety instructions. Never block ventilation pipes or hatches and, if you smell gas, make sure you do not use any form of flame or electrical switch and call the gas emergency service listed in the telephone book immediately.

10.3   Culture shock and its symptoms

When you leave a familiar environment and go for an extended stay somewhere quite different, you are bound to experience a whole range of feelings. Many of these emotions will be unexpected and sometimes very strong, making you feel out of control and confused. This is the experience we call culture shock, but you don't have to move from an entirely different culture to experience it. All students from overseas, even those coming from countries with very similar ways of life to those in Britain, can experience culture shock in some form. This is because there will always be some features of life that are different; also you are removed from the family and friends who normally support you through new or difficult experiences. An important factor that contributes to an initial sense of confusion is that you will probably find that the people you are working and living with are not aware of your feelings and may appear not to understand your anxieties.

Some of the differences can cause you practical anxieties – the fact that in Britain we drive on the left, for example. But even quite small differences such as the non-availability of certain foods or the fact that shops have different opening times can all contribute to making you feel disoriented in the short term. The important point to try to remember is that these are perfectly normal reactions and they will disappear as you become more accustomed to your new way of life. For those coming from a society with very different customs and behaviour patterns from Britain, the impact of culture shock may be more pronounced as you find all your expectations about people and their behaviour are no longer met. Common areas of difference are:

- modes of dress;
- behaviour considered appropriate to men and to women;
- aspects of religious practice;
- food and eating habits;
- climate.

At the beginning you are likely to feel excited by the new experience of coming to study in another country and you will be looking forward to arriving and meeting new people and starting your course. Quite quickly, however, you may find that the new experiences begin to overwhelm you and you begin to experience distressing emotions that might be unfamiliar to you. What you first found exciting may now seem alien, even frightening, and you will be wishing you were back among the familiar places and people at home. You may find that you are experiencing sudden mood changes and strong reactions to apparently trivial events. This is perhaps the most difficult phase for any new student and it is important to try to remember that what you are feeling is normal and that it will pass.

However, if you find yourself feeling unable to cope, do go to see the student counsellor or your personal tutor at your place of study and seek help. Because Britain welcomes many thousands of international students each year, universities and colleges employ professional counsellors and tutors, with special training in offering advice and support, to help students overcome their initial emotional and practical difficulties. These people understand the difficulties you may be having and will listen to you sympathetically.

Many people find that it helps to make contact with others of their own nationality. Although, objectively, you may not wish to seek out your compatriots, especially if you are trying to avoid speaking your own language in order to improve your English, it will help you at this stage to look for their support. People from a similar back-ground to your own will understand your reactions to the new environment. They will be able to talk about what is happening back home and they will make you feel less cut off and less a stranger. You will be able to cook your national food together, listen to familiar music, exchange newspapers and books and discuss the different aspects of British culture that you find difficult to accept.

It is not possible to say how long these different phases will take, as so much depends on individual reactions and the extent of the differences between the cultures you are experiencing. But try to remember that it is quite natural for you to go through stages of rejecting all that you find – the food, the mode of dress, the behaviour patterns, the climate – but as time goes on, you will gradually learn to re-evaluate them, finding some of them more acceptable than you first realized.

10.4   Cultural and religious differences

For those students unused to the kind of liberal Western culture that characterizes Britain, there will be all kinds of differences in daily life on a minor and a major level that can cause difficulties at times. If there are problems that cause you deep concern, then you will need to seek the support the advice of those who understand your point of view. However, the checklist below is designed to help you think about the significance of the differences you may find, and to work out whether they are likely to affect you deeply or not.

Many of these points are not things we think about in our own environment because we take it for granted that everyone behaves in a similar way. Even if some of the things mentioned are not really very important, the fact that they are different might cause you to feel uncomfortable and out of place.

General points
- How important is it to be punctual in your country? What have you noticed about punctuality in Britain?
- How do people greet each other in Britain? Is this different from what you are used to?

Accommodation
- Do you find that the heating is turned off at night? Does this cause you problems?

- Are you expected to make your own bed or do the washing up?
- Are there pets in the house where you are lodging? How do you feel about that? Have you discussed your feelings with your landlord/landlady?

Male and female roles

- Is there the same measure of sexual equality in your country as in Britain?
- Are you comfortable in mixed company?
- Are you comfortable having to live and study in close proximity to members of the opposite sex? Will this affect your work?
- Do you feel confident about how to dress?
- Do you find the way British people dress acceptable? If not, what is it that upsets you?
- Do you know how to greet someone of the opposite sex without appearing too friendly or too distant?

Politeness

- Do you feel that you understand the rules of politeness here?
- Are the customs of thanking, offering, accepting and refusing hospitality very different?
- Do you know when to buy gifts?
- Do you know which gestures and facial expressions seem impolite in this country?
- Do you feel comfortable when people ask you for your opinions?
- Do you know which personal questions are considered impolite in Britain? For example, it is not usually acceptable to ask people their age or how much they earn.

Food

- Do the people you socialize and mix with understand which foods you may and may not eat?
- Are you aware of the different methods of preparing food so that you can know if something is acceptable to you or not?
- At what time do you eat your main meal in your country? Is it very different here?

Religious or cultural practices

If you are staying in private accommodation, it is important to explain politely to your hosts any customs which you wish them to respect while you are staying with them. This may involve a need to be able to wash under running water, or to observe taboos on foods, a wish for privacy to pray or special times for eating. People will normally respect your practices but are not necessarily likely to know about them unless you inform them. It is helpful if you bring photographs and postcards from your own country to help friends and colleagues here visualize your home environment and understand that you are used to a different climate, different foods and different customs.

10.5   Personal safety

One of the problems associated with coming into a new environment is that you are not immediately aware of situations that might be dangerous. Personal safety in Britain is largely a matter of common sense. Big cities and crowded places have higher risks than small villages; being out at night is more dangerous than being out during the day. Under certain circumstances women need to take extra care to ensure that they are not travelling alone at night. Below are some points to bear in mind to protect yourself and your possessions.

Pickpockets are a feature of crowded places, especially airports, stations and crowded streets. Do no carry large amounts of cash. Report any theft of credit cards or passport to the police at once. Notify your bank immediately if credit cards and bank cards are stolen. Keep PINs separately from your cards and have a note of your personal card numbers and passport number filed safely where you are staying so that you can give full details when you report loss. *Mugging (street robbery)* is also associated with large cities. Avoid dark and lonely streets and subways. If threatened, hand over your money without a struggle. Report the incident to the police at once. Report the loss of any credit or cheque cards to your bank at once. As a precaution, never carry large amounts of cash with you.

Cars should never be left unlocked. Put all property in the boot of the car. Never leave anything valuable in a car. It may be too expensive to fit an alarm to your car but you can buy inexpensive clamps to fit to the steering wheel.

Sexual assault or harassment is feared by both young women and young men. You are vulnerable mainly when travelling alone, especially at night. Under those circumstances, be cautious about speaking to strangers, carry a personal alarm (weapons and chemical sprays are illegal) and avoid dark places such as subways.

Traffic in cities is heavy and drivers are often impatient so use pedestrian crossings. Take care to look both ways before crossing a road as traffic may be approaching from an unexpected direction.

Drugs, with the exception of remedies available over the counter such as paracetamol and aspirin, are illegal in Britain except on prescription by a doctor for medical use. Although the courts may give lighter penalties for the personal use of soft drugs such as cannabis, these are illegal, as well as the hard drugs such as cocaine. The courts are particularly severe on those they judge to be sellers or dealers. Drug 'pushers' operate in places where young people are likely to gather and students are always a special target.

10.6   How to ask for help

Below are suggestions for ways of obtaining help with specific difficulties as they arise.

Thefts or assaults: these should be reported to the police. If you need to call the police in an emergency, then telephone 999 (no money needed) and ask for the police service.

Homesickness, general feelings of being unable to cope: ask to see the student counsellor to discuss the specific causes of your problems. Many colleges and universities have a counsellor concerned specifically with helping international students to settle in. The counsellor will help with practical suggestions and, if necessary, will refer you to other professionals you may need to see.

Loneliness: find out if there are any societies for your nationality in your place of study or in your town. Ask the students' union to put you in contact with fellow nationals. Join societies in the university or in the town that cater for your leisure and sporting interests. When you have contact with fellow nationals, find out where you can buy foods that you eat at home, buy newspapers from your country and take the opportunity to share experiences and feelings with them.

Opportunities for worship: every major religion in the world is represented in Britain and most major cities have Muslim, Hindu, Sikh and Buddhist centres in addition to churches of all denominations and synagogues. Ask your students' union about finding a place of worship if you are not sure where to go

10.7   Climate and weather

One of the main features of the British climate is its variability. This means that even in summer there can be spells of cold, wet and windy weather. On the other hand it can mean that winters may be short and not very cold. Bear in mind also that there are regional variations in climate despite the relatively small size of the country. In general the west of Britain is wetter and milder than the east. In some parts of Scotland the winters can produce months of snow, while in the south snow is often not seen at all from one year to another.

Daylight hours

In Britain GMT (Greenwich Mean Time) applies in winter only. From March to October the clocks are altered for British Summer Time (BST). The result is that in June and July the south of England enjoys about sixteen hours of daylight but only eight hours during December and January. However, there are regional differences, with the north of Scotland having longer hours of daylight in the summer but shorter days in the winter.

Average temperatures and rainfall for London

(Average daily temperatures in centigrade and average monthly rainfall in millimetres)

Degrees C	Jan	Feb	Mar	Apr	May	Jun	Jul	Aug	Sep	Oct	Nov	Dec
	5	5	8	11	14	17	18	18	16	12	9	6
Rainfall	54	40	37	37	46	45	57	59	49	57	64	48

Regional variations

Average summer temperatures in Edinburgh are 12.9° C and in Manchester, 15.1° C, while in winter they are 2.3° C in Edinburgh and 3.00° C in Manchester. As you can see this is quite a big difference from London.

10.8 Festivals and special occasions

Christmas

Christmas is above all a family festival in Britain. 25 and 26 December are national holidays and on Christmas Day (25 December) it is traditional for families to congregate and celebrate Christmas lunch or dinner. Gifts are exchanged and, if you are staying with a British family, they will probably expect you to join in even if you are not a Christian. There is no public transport on Christmas Day and limited transport on Boxing Day (26 December). Although it is a religious festival and churches have special services, by no means everyone goes to church.

New Year's Day

1 January is also a public holiday and many people stay up until beyond midnight on 31 December to welcome the New Year. In Scotland this is an even more festive occasion than Christmas (known as Hogmanay)

Easter

Easter does not have fixed dates but is between late March and mid-April. The public holiday extends from good Friday to Easter Monday. Again there are special church services. Children receive gifts of chocolate eggs and there are Easter parades in many towns on Easter Sunday. On the Thursday before Easter, the Queen visits a different cathedral each year to give a symbolic gift of money (Maundy money) to local inhabitants.

Guy Fawkes Night

5 November is not a public holiday, but all over Britain there are bonfires and fireworks to celebrate the foiling of the Gunpowder Plot on Parliament in 1605. Celebrations are particularly spectacular in Lewes, East Sussex and Ottery St Mary in Devon.

Apart from these major occasions, there is a series of annual events that help give the visitor a flavour of British life – both traditional and ethnic. Some of these are shown below.

Public Holidays for 1996 are:
- New Year (1 January)
- Good Friday (5 April)
- Easter Monday (8 April)
- Bank Holiday (6 May)
- Bank Holiday (27 May)
- Bank Holiday (26 August)
- Christmas Day (25 December)
- Boxing Day (26 December)

Scotland has an additional Bank Holiday on 2 January and Northern Ireland an additional Bank Holiday on 18 March.

February	**The Chinese New Year** is celebrated in London's Chinatown and other major towns – e.g. Manchester – with Chinese communities.
	Shrove Tuesday (the day before Lent) is celebrated by eating pancakes but also by pancake races.
March	**The Grand National** horse race takes place at Aintree, Liverpool.
April	**The Cambridge/Oxford Boat Race** (a boat race between crews from the Universities of Oxford and Cambridge) takes place on the River Thames in London.
	The London Marathon is run in late April.
May	**May Day** is celebrated in country areas by morris dancing and dancing round the maypole.
	The FA Cup Final takes place in early May at Wembley Stadium in London.

The Chelsea Flower Show takes place over four days in late May.

The **Glyndebourne** opera season begins at Glyndebourne near Lewes in Sussex.

June

12 June: **Trooping the Colour** at Buckingham Palace.

Two major horse-racing events take place in June: **The Derby** in the first week and **Royal Ascot** in the last.

The Wimbledon Lawn Tennis Championships begin in the last week of June.

July

The Henley Regatta takes place in early July on the River Thames in Oxfordshire.

The British Open Golf Championship takes place in mid-July at a different golf course each year.

The Royal Tournament takes place at Earls Court in the last week of July.

The annual season of **Henry Wood Promenade Concerts** begins at the Albert Hall in late July.

August

Cowes Week on the Isle of Wight is a yachting and sailing event taking place in early August.

Edinburgh Military Tattoo takes place in early August and the Edinburgh International Arts Festival and Fringe Festival begins at about the same time.

The Notting Hill Carnival takes place on Bank Holiday Monday in West London. It is a celebration organized by London's Caribbean community.

September	**Blackpool's illuminations** begin in early September, providing five miles of exotic lights.
	Southampton International Boat Show takes place in late September.
	Soho Jazz Festival.
	Wigan Jazz Festival.
October	**The Huddersfield Contemporary Music Festival** begins in late October.
November	**The London to Brighton Veteran Car Rally** takes place.
	The Lord Mayor's Procession and Show takes place in mid-November.

10.9   Exploring and travelling in Britain

Britain can offer such diversity of landscapes and such a range of architectural styles that most visitors coming for an extended stay will wish to explore the country. There are many miles of coastal paths; there are mountainous districts in Wales, Scotland, the Lake District and the Peak District. There is agricultural land and forest and many acres of national parks where visitors can ramble or watch birds. Of course there are also major cities such as Manchester and Birmingham as well as capital cities of London, Edinburgh, Cardiff and Belfast, all offering sophisticated shops, restaurants, cultural pursuits and night life. Important too are the famous university towns of Oxford, Cambridge and St Andrews, which must surely be of interest to international students. Smaller towns are also worth investigating as nearly every town in Britain has something of interest for the visitors.

ℹ With such a choice of activity, the first step is to find the information you need about different areas and how to reach them. Your local tourist information office will be able to help, so will the regional tourist offices for the areas you wish to visit. There is also the national Tourist Information Centre at Victoria Station in London. Local travel agents will have brochures giving information about breaks in different parts of Britain and the *Radio Times* has a regular tourism feature giving details of leaflets and brochures available, as do most of the Sunday newspapers.

ℹ️ Fortunately travel by coach and bus is comparatively cheap and it is also possible to find inexpensive accommodation. Youth hostels are probably the best value for money, but accommodation can often be basic and you may have to be willing to sleep in a dormitory or to

 share rooms. A list of youth hostels and their regulations can be obtained from the Youth Hostels Association (the address is given at the end of the chapter). In big towns you may be able to find rooms in hostels such as the YMCA or student hostels (see Appendix 2). Apart from these options, many private guest houses offer inexpensive accommodation on a 'bed and breakfast' basis. If you are able to travel outside the main holiday seasons, you will also find that hotels offer cheap weekend stays or even longer breaks. The British Tourist Authority supplies a leaflet called 'Meet the British' listing agencies and individual families offering private accommodation. Camping and caravanning are other ways of exploring the countryside inexpensively. If you are camping independently, make sure you pitch your tent only in an official camp site or somewhere where you have the permission of the landowner.

Don't forget to check with your students' union to see if there are any trips or excursions being specially organized for students at favourable rates.

One final word about the mode of travel. The network of train and bus services should give you access to any of the places you wish to visit. Obviously the use of a car makes your travelling even more flexible. Hitch-hiking, however, is not recommended. Nowadays, motorists feel unsafe in offering lifts to strangers and women hitch-hikers in particular are vulnerable to attack or abduction. This form of travel is not illegal in Britain but it is not to be advised. If you are determined to hitch-hike, then it would be wiser to travel with a companion than alone and to leave details of your destination and timetable with a friend or your tutor.

Country code

Many visitors will wish to spend time in the countryside for
pleasure. If you do so, you should pay attention to the voluntary
'country code' that offers good advice for responsible enjoyment of
country pursuits:

- Don't light fires or start fires accidentally.
- Take your litter home with you.
- Always keep to public footpaths and close all gates behind you.
- Don't interfere with farm equipment or animals.
- Keep dogs under control at all times.
- Make no unnecessary noise.
- Respect the wildlife, and take no birds' eggs or wild flowers.

10.10 Travelling to neighbouring countries

Britain is obviously a useful starting-point for exploring other
European countries and your students' union will have details of
special students' fares. One popular way of travelling around Europe
is with an Inter-Rail card which costs (currently) £180 and provides
one month's travel in twenty-four countries. There are also many
discount air fares for students and many travel agents have details of
inexpensive package tours. Now that the Channel Tunnel is open, it
is also possible to travel direct by train to Paris and Brussels.

If you do plan to leave Britain, you will have to check whether you
need visas to enter the countries you wish to visit. If you needed a
visa to enter Britain and your stay in Britain is under six months you
should have a multiple entry visa to enable you to return to Britain.
Without this, you will have to apply for a new entry visa in the
country you are visiting and there is no guarantee that such a visa
will be issued. If you are a visa-national and your course is longer
than six months, you do not need a multiple-entry visa to come back
to Britain within the duration of your course. You should, however,
have a document that confirms where you are a full-time student.

10.11 Sources of information

Addresses of organizations mentioned in this chapter
The British Tourist Authority, Thames Tower, Blacks Road, Hammersmith, London SW1 4PQ, Tel: (0) 171-846 9000.

The Tourist Information Centre (LTB), Victoria Station, London SW1V 1JU, Tel: (0) 171-730 3488.

Youth Hostels Association (YHA) National Office, 8 St Stephens Hill, St Albans, Hertfordshire AL1 2DY, Tel: (0) 1727 855215.

Further reading
Britain: an official handbook, HMSO: Foreign and Commonwealth Office, £21.00, annual.

Fodor's Great Britain, Random Century, annual, £13.99.

Mikes, G. *How to be a Brit*, Penguin, 1986, £5.99.

Young Britain British Tourist Authority Annual, free.

11 Preparing to go home

In this chapter we look at preparation and your possible experiences on going back to your own country. After a prolonged stay in Britain, you will need to make practical arrangements for your return to your home country. However, you will also need to prepare yourself mentally and emotionally because your experience in a new environment will have had an impact on your ideas and your feelings. The person returning will not be quite the same person who arrived.

'After a lengthy stay, you will have accumulated quite a lot ...'

11.1 Preparing for packing and luggage

Inevitably after a lengthy stay, you will have accumulated quite a lot of possessions, some of which you will wish to take home and others which are better left behind. The following points should be considered before you pack:

- Have you acquired/bought items that you are not allowed to take back to your country?
- Have you items on which you will be charged excise duties?
- Have you taken advantage of VAT exemption for overseas visitors on buying any large or expensive items? If so, will you have to pay VAT on them in your own country?
- Have you weighed your luggage to see if you will incur excess baggage charges?
- Is it worth sending any major items home through a freight company?

● Can you sell items such as books and, perhaps, heavy winter clothing to other students?

11.2   Saying goodbye to friends and colleagues

If you have spent a lengthy period of time working alongside colleagues and friends, don't forget to make a point of seeing them to say goodbye. The student counsellor and academic staff will appreciate a personal visit to know your future plans and give you their good wishes. They may even be able to help you with some of the arrangements for your departure. Friends will want to have a contact address for you in the future.

'Don't forget to say goodbye to friends and colleagues'

11.3   Culture shock in reverse

Just as you will have looked forward to your visit to Britain with a mixture of apprehension and excitement, so you will think about returning home in just the same way. You will probably be glad to be able to go back to your family and friends and there may be aspects of life at home that you will have really missed and look forward to enjoying again. However, you will also feel regret at leaving your new friends and colleagues and you may feel that you will miss life at college or university with all its opportunities for a diverse social and cultural life. You should not be surprised, therefore, if you begin to experience conflicting emotions just after you return home in much the same way as you did when you first came to Britain. You will feel different and you will experience your home surroundings, however familiar they are to you, in a different way.

Some of the points to be aware of:

● You will seem different to the people at home – perhaps more sophisticated, perhaps less accepting of all that you find around you.
● You will re-evaluate your own culture in terms of what you have experienced elsewhere. Some things will seem more important than before, others less so.
● You may not have as much freedom as you did when you were a student in Britain.
● People may not react to you as you would wish. They may, for example, be less interested in hearing about your experiences abroad than you think. To them, your life in Britain may seem remote and irrelevant to their own situation. Other people may feel you have become more important, less approachable than before you obtained impressive qualifications. Others, again, may be envious of your opportunities and be less than friendly than before.

11.4 Settling back into family, social life and work

You may have to give yourself time to readjust to the new old life. It may be helpful to contact other people who have shared your experiences and have developed broader horizons themselves. It may take time to reassure your family and friends that you have not changed fundamentally. You may find it difficult to settle back into your old style of life. If you have been used to spending leisure time with friends doing what you wanted to do whenever you chose, it may be hard to find yourself having to account for your companions to parents. Equally, you may find your friends are not as free as you have become and they may be reluctant to share your new attitudes.

At work, you may find routines more rigid and disciplined than you had imagined, especially after the freedom of the student lifestyle. You may also find some resistance to new ideas and practices that you have learnt and wish to implement. It is important to remember that you have had to change a lot in a short time, whereas at home things will have been developing at their normal pace and not everyone will be ready to accept what might, to them, seem like major innovations.

11.5 Coping with changes

You may be surprised also to find how much has changed. There may be new political structures, new laws. You may find yourself plunged into a new and demanding job or you may find that, despite your new qualifications, you cannot find a job at once. There will be changes too among your family and friends. People will have married, children may have been born, some people may have died, others may have moved away and new people may have moved back into your circle. Changes such as these can confuse and make you feel insecure at first.

It might also be hard to deal with the expectations others now have of you, especially your family. For many families, sending someone abroad to study can entail financial as well as emotional investment. They may have expectations that you in some way will return this investment by being successful in your career and showing your gratitude. They may also wish to display their pride in you and hold parties and social gatherings in your honour.

All this may be almost more of a culture shock than that of visiting a foreign country, because you feel your home environment should be thoroughly familiar to you. The important point to remember is that, just as initial culture shock is an entirely normal reaction, so 'reverse culture shock' is equally normal. You may find that you go through the following phases:

- Excitement at the prospect of going home.
- Rapidly changing emotions as you cope with changes and find out how different reality is from your expectation.
- Gradual re-acceptance of the home culture.
- Ultimately, a broader perspective in which you can appreciate what is valuable, but be aware of the limitations of the two backgrounds you now know.

Appendix 1

Other useful addresses and sources of advice

A Education and qualifications in general

The British Council
10 Spring Gardens
London SW1A 2BN
Telephone: (0) 171-930 8466
Fax: (0) 171-839 6347
(Information Centre – personal callers welcome)

The British Council
Medlock Street
Manchester M15 4AA
Telephone: (0) 161-957 7755
Fax: (0) 161-957 7762
(Information Centre – personal callers welcome)

The British Council's Head Office is located on two sites, Manchester and London. The British Council has other offices in most major cities worldwide.

The Department for Education and Employment
Sanctuary Buildings
Great Smith Street
London SW1P 3BT
Telephone: (0) 171-925 5000
Fax: (0) 171-925 6000
(General information about education in Britain)

Engineering Careers Information Service
41 Clarendon Road
Watford
Hertfordshire WD1 1HS
Telephone: freephone (0) 800 282167
Fax: (0) 1923 256086
(Information on courses in engineering)

Gabbitas, Truman and Thring Educational Trust
Carrington House
126–130 Regent Street
London W1R 6EE
Telephone: (0) 171-734 0161
Fax: (0) 171-437 1764
(Information about independent public schools in Britain)

Information Technology Training Accreditation Council
IDPM House
Edgington Way
Ruxley Corner
Sidcup
Kent DA14 5HR
Telephone: (0) 181-309 5496
Fax: (0) 181-308 0604
(Information on approved training in IT)

The International Baccalaureate Office
Pascal Close
St Mellons
Cardiff CF3 0YP
Telephone: (0) 1222 770770
Fax: (0) 1222 770333
(Information on the IB examinations)

The Law Society
Careers Office
227–228 Strand
London WC2R 1BA
Telephone: (0) 171-242 1222
Fax: (0) 171-583 5531
(Information on courses and qualifications in law)

The National Advice Centre for Postgraduate Dental Education
Faculty of Dental Surgery
Royal College of Surgeons of England
35–43 Lincoln's Inn Fields
London WC2A 3PN
Telephone: (0) 171-405 3474
Fax: (0) 171-831 9438
(Information on dentistry training)

The National Advice Centre for Postgraduate Medical Education
Third Floor
The British Council
Medlock Street
Manchester M15 4AA
Telephone: (0) 161-957 7218
Fax: (0) 161-957 7724

The National Council for Vocational Qualifications
222 Euston Road
London NW1 2BZ
Telephone: (0) 171-387 9898
Fax: (0) 171-387 0978
(Information about GNVQs)

The UK Central Council for Nursing, Midwifery and Health Visiting
23 Portland Place
London W1N 4JT
Telephone: (0) 171-637 7181
Fax: (0) 171-436 2924
(Information about post-basic nursing training)

B Accommodation, student welfare and other general information

Alcoholics Anonymous
PO Box 1
Stonebow House
Stonebow
York YO1 2NJ
Telephone: (0) 1904 644026
Fax: (0) 1904 629091
London helpline: (0) 171-352 3001
(Support centre for people with drinking problems)

International Students House (ISH)
229 Great Portland Street
London W1N 5HD
Telephone: (0) 171-631 3223
Fax: (0) 171-631 8315
(Club and accommodation centre for international students in London)

Joint Council for the Welfare of Immigrants
115 Old Street
London EC1V 9JR
Telephone: (0) 171-251 8706
Fax: (0) 171-251 5110
(Advice on immigration matters)

Law Centres Federation
Duchess House
18–19 Warren Street
London W1P 5DB
Telephone: (0) 171-387 8570
Fax: (0) 171-387 8368
(Provides list of local law centres throughout Britain where free legal advice can be obtained)

The London Tourist Board
26 Grosvenor Gardens
London SW1W 0DU
Telephone: (0) 171-730 3450/3488
Fax: (0) 171-730 9367
(General tourist information about London)

National Council of YMCAs
640 Forest Road
London E17 3DZ
Telephone: (0) 181-520 5599
Fax: (0) 181-509 3190
(General information on YMCAs)

The Terrence Higgins Trust
52–54 Gray's Inn Road
London W1X 8JU
Telephone: (0) 171-242 1010
(helpline, 12.00 p.m–10.00 p.m.)
(0) 171-405 2381
*(legal line, Mon.–Wed., 7.00 p.m.–
9.00 p.m.)*
Fax: (0) 171-242 0121
(Help and information about Aids)

**UKCOSA: The Council for
International Education**
9–17 St Albans Place
London N1 0NX
Telephone: (0) 171-226 3762
(general information)
(0) 171-354 5210

(help and advice line)
Fax: (0) 171-226 3373
*(Information and advice on a
variety of matters concerning
international students in Britain)*

World University Service
20 Compton Terrace
London N1 2UN
Telephone: (0) 171-226 6747
Fax: (0) 171-226 0482
*(Information about financial
assistance for refugee students, or
for students in financial difficulty
due to changed political circumstances in their home country)*

The Youth Hostels Association
Trevelyan House
8 St Stephen's Hill
St Albans
Hertfordshire AL1 2DY
Telephone: (0) 1727 855215
Fax: (0) 1727 844126

Appendix 2

Student hostel addresses

M = men, W = women, MC =
married couples, Ch = children,
PG Med = postgraduate medical
students only, PG = postgraduate

London area

AFSIL Ltd (M, W, MC, Ch)
10 Endsleigh Gardens
London WC1H 0EN
Telephone: (0) 171-388 7144
Fax: (0) 171-383 5462
*Full-time postgraduates attending
the LSE, LSHTM, RPMS, SOAS
and UCL only.*

Alliance Club (M)
44–45 Newington Green
London N16 9QH
Telephone: (0) 171-226 6085
Fax: (0) 171-704 2486

Annesley House (W)
2 Princes Way
London SW19 6QE
Telephone: (0) 181-788 9737

Arthur West House (M, W, MC)
79 Fitzjohns Avenue
London NW3 6PA
Telephone: (0) 171-435 8793
Fax: (0) 171-431 7873

Ashwell House (W)
10 Wellesley Terrace
London N1 7NA
Telephone: (0) 171-490 5021
Fax: (0) 171-336 6433

Barnet Overseas Student Housing Association (MC,Ch)
Nansen Village
21 Woodside Avenue
London N12 8AQ
Telephone: (0) 181-445 8644
Fax: (0) 181-343 8667

Bartrams Hostel (W)
Rowland Hill Street
London NW3 5JA
Telephone: (0) 171-431 5680
Fax: (0) 171-794 8644

Bernard Johnson House (MC,Ch, PG Med)
78 Fortis Green
East Finchley
London N2 9EX
Telephone: (0) 181-883 4336

Catholic Students International (M)
International Chaplaincy
16C Portland Rise
London N4 2PP
Telephone: (0) 181-802 9673
Fax: (0) 181-802 9673

Centre Français (M, W, Ch)
61/9 Chepstow Place
London W2 4TR
Telephone: (0) 171-221 8134
Fax: (0) 171-221 0652

Chester House Hostel (M, W)
1 Chester House
Pages Lane
Muswell Hill
London N10 1PR
Telephone: (0) 181-883 8204
Fax: (0) 181-365 2471

Christian Alliance Centre (M,W)
Secker Street
London SE1 8UF
Telephone: (0) 171-633 0128
Fax: (0) 171-401 9945

Clubland Methodist Hostel (M,W)
56 Camberwell Road
London SE5 0EN
Telephone: (0) 171-701 0233

Croydon YMCA (M, W)
1 Lansdowne Road
Croydon CR0 2BX
Telephone: (0) 181-681 3381
Fax: (0) 181-686 9461

Fellowship House (M,W, MC)
Mecklenburgh Square
London WC1N 2AB
Telephone: (0) 171-837 8888
Fax: (0) 171-837 9321

Gilmore House (MC, Ch)
113 Clapham Common
North Side
London SW4 9SJ
Telephone: (0) 171-228 2130

Impala House (M, MC, W, Ch)
8 Chalcot Square
London NW1 8YB
Telephone: (0) 171-916 5415
Fax: (0) 171-916 5415

International House (M,F, MC,Ch)
109 Brookhill Road
London SE18 6RZ
Telephone: (0) 181-854 1418
Fax: (0) 181-855 9257

International Students Hostel (W)
Frognal House
99 Frognal
London NW3 6XR
Telephone: (0) 171-794 6893

International Students House (M, W, MC, Ch)
229 Great Portland Street
London W1N 5HD
Telephone: (0) 171-631 2300
Fax: (0) 171-631 8315

Jerome House (M,W, MC, Ch)
5–13 Glendower Place
London SW7 3DU
Telephone: (0) 171-584 2906
Fax: (0) 171-589 3648
Postgraduates from the
Commonwealth or developing
countries preferred.

Kingston upon Thames
Churches Housing Association
(M,W)
Meadway House
17–21 Brighton Road, Surbiton
Surrey KT6 5LR
Telephone: (0) 181-399 7221

Lee Abbey International
Students Club (M, W)
57–64 Lexham Gardens
London W8 6JJ
Telephone: (0) 171-373 7242
Fax: (0) 171-244 8702

Leinster House (M, W)
46 Leinster Gardens
London W2 3AT
Telephone: (0) 171-723 7803
Fax: (0) 171-262 3794

Lilian Penson Hall
(University of London)
(M, W, MC)
Talbot Square
London W2 1TT
Telephone: (0) 171-262 2081
Fax: (0) 171-724 1258

London Friendship Centre
(M,W)
'Peace Haven'
3 Creswick Road
London W3 9HE
Telephone: (0) 181-992 0221
Fax: (0) 181-992 0221

London Goodenough Trust
Mecklenburgh Square
London WC1N 2AB
Telephone: (0) 171-837 8888
Fax: (0) 171-837 932
Fellowship House
(M, W, MC)
London House
(M, W, MC)
William Goodenough House
(M, W, MC, Ch)
Commonwealth, ex-
Commonwealth, US and European
postgraduate students

YWCA
Helen Graham House (M, W)
184 Tottenham Lane
London N8 8SG
Telephone: (0) 181 340 2345
Fax: (0) 181-340 2345

Methodist International House
2 Inverness Terrace
London W2 3HY
Telephone: (0) 171-229 5101
Fax: (0) 171-229 3170

The Moullin House (M, W)
24–26 Mount Park Road
Ealing
London W5 2RT
Telephone: (0) 181-997 4343
Fax: (0) 181-991 0254

Nansen Village (MC, Ch)
21 Woodside Avenue
London N12 8QA
Telephone: (0) 181 445 8644
Fax: (0) 181-343 8667

Sentosa House (M,W, MC, Ch)
15/19 Upper Montague Street
London W1H 1RR
Telephone: (0) 171-402 5757

Netherhall House (M)
Nutley Terrace
London NW3 5SA
Telephone: (0) 171-435 8888
Fax: (0) 171-894 2442

Park House YWCA (W)
227 Earls Court Road
London SW5 9BL
Telephone: (0) 171-373 2851
Fax: (0) 171-370 5275

Princess House YWCA (W)
39 Ennismore Gardens
London SW7 1AG
Telephone: (0) 171-584 3060
Shared accommodation only

Friendship House (M,MC,Ch)
1 St Nicholas Glebe
Rectory Lane
London SW17 9QH
Telephone: (0) 181-672 2262
Fax: (0) 181-672 2921

London Student Housing
1 St Nicholas Glebe
Rectory Lane
London SW17 9QH
Telephone: (0) 181-672 2262
Fax: (0) 181-672 2921

Queen Alexandra's House
Kensington Gore
London SW7 2QT
Telephone: (0) 171-589 1120
Fax: (0) 171-589 3177

Religious of Mary Immaculate (W)
Struan House
44 Augustus Road
London SW19 6NB
Telephone: (0) 181 788 9477

Romford YMCA (M, W)
Rush Green Road
Romford
Essex RM7 0PH
Telephone: (0) 708 766211
Fax: (0) 1708 754211

Rothamsted Overseas Housing Association (M, W, MC, Ch)
Rothamsted Experimental Station
Harpenden
Hertfordshire AL5 2JQ
Telephone: (0) 15827 63133
Fax: (0) 15827 63133

Salvation Army (W)
Hopetown
60 Old Montague Street
London E1 5NG
Telephone: (0) 171-247 1004

Sisters of St Dorothy International Students Hostel (W)
Frognal House
99 Frognal
Hampstead
London NW3 6XR
Telephone: (0)171-794 6893/8095

Thompson House (M, W)
583 Commercial Road
London E1 0HJ
Telephone: (0) 171-790 3366

The Victoria League Students House (M,W, MC)
55 Leinster Square
London W2 4PU
Telephone: (0) 171-229 3961
Fax: (0) 171-229 2994
Commonwealth students under the age of 30

Waltham Forest YMCA (M, W, MC)
Charter House
Charter Place
Watford WD1 2RT
Telephone: (0) 1923 233034
Fax: (0) 1923 226299

William Temple House (M, W)
29 Trebovir Road
London SW5 9NF
Telephone: (0) 171-373 6962
Fax: (0) 171-373 6972

Wimbledon YMCA (M, W)
200 The Broadway
Wimbledon
London SW19 1RY
Telephone: (0) 181-542 9055
Fax: (0) 181-542 1086

Zebra Housing Association (M, W, MC, Ch)
5 Glendower Place
London SW7 3DU
Telephone: (0) 171-584 2906
Fax: (0) 171-589 3648

Hostels for nationals

Austria

Austrian Catholic Centre (F)
29 Brooke Green
London W6 8BL
Telephone: (0) 171-603 2697

Denmark

Danish YMCA
43 Maresfield Gardens
London NW3 5TF
Telephone: (0) 171-435 2007
Fax: (0) 171-431 1394
Preference given to Danish men and women. All shared rooms. Tube station: Finchley Road.

France

The French Centre
61–69 Chepstow Place
London W2 4TR
Telephone: (0) 171-221 8134
Fax: (0) 171-221 0652
Men and women of all nationalities. Tube station: Earls Court.

Germany

German YMCA
35 Craven Terrace
Lancaster Gate
London W2 3EL
Telephone: (0) 171-723 9276
Fax: (0) 171-706 2870
Men and women of all nationalities. Tube station: Earl's Court.

India

Indian Students Hostel
41 Fitzroy Square
London W1P 6AQ
Telephone: (0) 171-387 0411
Fax: (0) 171-383 7651
Men and women of all nationalities. Tube station: Great Portland Street or Warren Street.

Malaysia

Malaysia Hall
46 Bryanston Square
London W1H 8AJ
Telephone: (0) 171-723 9484
Fax: (0) 171-706 4721
Only Malaysian men and women. Office: 44 Bryanston Square. Tube station: Marble Arch.

Muslim Hostel
38 Matesbury Road
London NW2 4JD
Telephone: (0) 181-452 9340
Fax: (0) 181-208 4161
Muslim men only. Tube station: Kilburn.

Poland

Polish YMCA
46/7 Kensington Gardens Square
London W2 4BQ
Telephone: (0) 171-229 4678
*Men and women of all
nationalities. Tube station:
Bayswater or Queensway.*

Other hostels in the UK

Aberdeen

Cameron House (W)
2–4 Charlotte Street
Aberdeen AB1 1LR
Telephone: (0) 1224 634966
Fax: (0) 1224 637561

Aviemore

Torr Lodge (M)
Morlich Court
Aviemore
Inverness-shire PH22 1SL
Telephone: (0) 1479 810150

Bath

City of Bath YMCA (M,W)
YMCA International House
Broad Street Place
Bath BA1 5LN
Telephone: (0) 1225 460471
Fax: (0) 1225 462065

Belfast

YWCA (M, W)
Queen Mary's Hostel
70 Fitzwilliam Street
Belfast BT9 6AX
Telephone: (0) 1232 240439

Birkenhead

YMCA (M, W)
56 Whetstone Lane
Birkenhead
Merseyside L41 2TJ
Telephone: (0) 151-647 8123
Fax: (0) 151-650 1944

Birmingham

**Methodist International House
(M, W, MC, no. Ch)**
52 Oakfield Road
Selly Park
Birmingham B29 7EQ
Telephone: (0) 121-472 0109

**Methodist Overseas Guest
House (M, W, MC, Ch)**
College Walk
Selly Oak
Birmingham B29 6LF
Telephone: (0) 121-472 0163

YMCA (M, W)
300 Reservoir Road
Erdington
Birmingham B23 6DB
Telephone: (0) 121-373 1937)
Fax: (0) 121-382 3746

Bournemouth

YMCA (M, W)
56 Westover Road
Bournemouth BH1 2BS
Telephone: (0) 1202 290451
Fax: (0) 1202 314219

Bristol

**Girls' Friendly Society
Housing Association (W)**
Townsend House
Pump Lane
Redcliffe
Bristol BS4 6NW
Telephone: (0) 117 9273844

Methodist International House (M, W)
Rodney House
Clifton Down Road
Clifton Village
Bristol BS8 4AL
Telephone: (0) 117 9735179

Zebra Trust (MC, Ch)
Zebra House
9 Miles Road
Clifton
Bristol BS8 2JN
Telephone: (0) 117 9738084

Cambridge

YMCA (M, W, MC)
Gonville Place
Cambridge CB1 1ND
Telephone: (0) 1223 356998
Fax: (0) 1223 312749

Cardiff

YMCA (M, W)
The Walk
Roath
Cardiff CF2 3AG
Telephone: (0) 1222 497044
Fax: (0) 1222-471826

Cheltenham

YMCA (M, W)
6 Vittoria Walk
Cheltenham
Gloucestershire GL50 1TP
Telephone: (0) 1242 524024
Fax: (0) 1242 232638

Dalkeith

Lauder Lodge (M)
Newmills Road
Dalkeith
Midlothian EH22 1DX
Telephone: (0) 131-6601069

Derby

YMCA (M, W)
London Road
Wilmorton
Derby DE24 8UT
Telephone: (0) 1332 572076
Fax: (0) 1332 572596

Edinburgh

Scottish Council YWCA Housing Society (M, W, Ch)
22 Rutland Square
Edinburgh EH1 2BB
Telephone: (0) 131-229 9765
Fax: (0) 131-229 8236
Flats for international students' families

YWCA
22 Rutland Square
Edinburgh EH1 2BB
Telephone: (0) 131-229 9765
Fax: (0) 131-229 8236

Exeter

YMCA (M, W)
39 St David's Hill
Exeter EX4 4DA
Telephone: (0) 1392 410530
Fax: (0) 1392 422536

Glasgow

YMCA (M, W, MC)
David Naismith Court
33 Petershill Drive
Glasgow G21 4QQ
Telephone: (0) 141-558 6166
Fax: (0) 141-558 5623

Nautical College (M, W)
21 Thistle Street
Glasgow G5 9XB
Telephone: (0) 141-429 2553
Fax: (0) 141-420 1690

Grimsby

**Grimsby Cleethorpes and
District YMCA**
Peaks Lane
Grimsby
South Humberside DN32 9ET
Telephone: (0) 1472 357788
Fax: (0) 1472 340086

Hull

**Hull Methodist International
House (M, W, MC)**
96–8 Westbourne Avenue
Hull HU5 3HY
Telephone: (0) 1482 342104
Fax: (0) 1482 447729Leicester

Kirkaldy YWCA Residence (W)
236 London Road
Leicester LE2 1RH
Telephone: (0) 116 2705085

Liverpool

YMCA (M, W, MC)
56–60 Mount Pleasant
Liverpool L3 5FH
Telephone: (0) 151-709 9516
Fax: (0) 151-708 0141

YPHA (M,W, MC)
7th Floor, Wellington Buildings
The Strand
Liverpool L2 0PP
Telephone: (0) 151-227 3716
Fax: (0) 151-255 0338

Loughborough

**International Centre
(Loughborough) Ltd**
94 Leicester Road
Loughborough
Leicestershire LE11 2AQ
Telephone: (0) 1509 216288

Manchester

**Methodist International House
(M, W)**
68 Daisy Bank Road
Victoria Park
Manchester M14 5QP
Telephone: (0) 161-224 8041
Fax: (0) 161-225 0823

Alexandra House (M, W)
73 Carlton Road
Whalley Range
Manchester M16 8BQ
Telephone: (0) 161-226 2768
Fax: (0) 161-226 2768

Newcastle upon Tyne

YWCA (M, W)
Jesmond House
Clayton Road
Newcastle upon Tyne NE2 1UJ
Telephone: (0) 191-281 5466
Fax: (0) 191 212 0070

Norwich

YMCA (M, W)
48 St Giles Street
Norwich NR2 1LP
Telephone: (0) 1603 620269
Fax: (0) 1603 768382

Nottingham

YMCA (M, W)
4 Shakespeare Street
Nottingham NG1 4FG
Telephone: (0) 115 9473068
Fax: (0) 115 9567600

Oxford

YWCA (W)
133 Woodstock Road
Oxford OX2 6HW
Telephone: (0) 1865 52021
Long term stay only

Plymouth

YWCA (M, W)
9–13 Lockyer Street
Plymouth PL1 2QQ
Telephone: (0) 1752 660321

Portsmouth and Southsea

YMCA (M, W)
Penny Street
Old Portsmouth PO1 2NN
Telephone: (0) 1705 864341
Fax: (0) 1705 293276

Reading

Foley Hall (M, MC)
58/60 London Road
Reading RG1 5AS
Telephone: (0) 1734 872280
Fax: (0) 1734 758445

Trinity Hall (M, W)
South Street,
Reading RG1 4QU
Telephone: (0) 1734 391013

YMCA (M, W)
Marlborough House
34 Parkside Road
Reading RG3 2DD
Telephone: (0) 1734 575746
Fax: (0) 1734 588684

Sheffield

YMCA (M, W, MC)
Broomhall Road
Sheffield S10 2DG
Telephone: (0) 114 2684807
Fax: (0) 114 2683472

Southampton

YMCA (M, W)
George Williams House
Cranbury Place, Inner Avenue
Southampton SO14 0LG
Telephone: (0) 1703 221202
Fax: (0) 1703 633412

YWCA
Princess Margaret House
5 Bellevue Road
Southampton SO15 2YE
Telephone: (0) 1703 227155

Taunton

YWCA Residential Club (W)
18 Mary Street
Taunton
Somerset TA1 3PE
Telephone: (0) 1823 284682

West Bromwich

**West Bromwich and District
YMCA (M, W)**
38 Carters Green
West Bromwich
West Midlands B70 9LG
Telephone: (0) 121-553 4211/2
Fax: (0) 121-580 0225

Wolverhampton

YWCA (W)
The Lindens and International
House
100 Penn Road
Woverhampton WV3 0DW
Telephone: (0) 1902 23733
(*The Lindens*)
(0) 1902 24596 (*International
House*)

York

**York Housing Association Ltd
(M, W, MC, Ch)**
2 Newgate
York YO1 2LA
Telephone: (0) 1904 636061
Fax: (0) 1904 612623

Appendix 3

UK higher education addresses

This list is intended to be a quick reference document including universities and colleges and institutes of higher education in Britain. It does not include specialist professional training institutions, though these may offer qualifications validated by one of the listed institutions.

Inclusion in this list is not synonymous with recognition of courses. *Recognised Degree Courses in the United Kingdom*, published by the Department for Education and Employment, and available for consultation at British Council offices, is the authoritative list of institutions authorized by the UK government to award degrees.

Universities

University of Aberdeen
Regent Walk
Old Aberdeen
Aberdeen AB9 1FX
Telephone: (0) 1224 272000
Fax: (0) 1224 272086
Telex: 73458 UNIABN G

University of Abertay, Dundee
Bell Street
Dundee DD1 1HG
Telephone: (0) 1382 308000
Fax: (0) 1382 308877

Anglia Polytechnic University
Victoria Road South
Chelmsford CM1 1LL
Telephone: (0) 1245 493131
Fax: (0) 1245 495419

Aston University
Aston Triangle
Birmingham B4 7ET
Telephone: (0) 121-359 3611
Fax: (0) 121-359 7358
Telex: 336997 UNIAST G

University of Bath
Claverton Down
Bath BA2 7AY
Telephone: (0) 1225 826826
Fax: (0) 1225 462508
Telex: 449097

Queen's University of Belfast
University Road
Belfast BT7 1NN
Telephone: (0) 1232 245133
Fax: (0) 1232 236618
Telex: 682475

University of Birmingham
Edgbaston
Birmingham B15 2TT
Telephone: (0) 121-414 3696
Fax: (0) 121-414 3850
Telex: 333762 UOBHAM G
E-mail: P.S.Jones@bham.ac.uk.

University of Central England in Birmingham
Perry Barr
Birmingham B42 2SU
Telephone: (0) 121-331-5000
Fax: (0) 121-356 2875

Bournemouth University
Talbot Campus
Fern Barrow
Poole
Dorset BH12 5BB
Telephone: (0) 1202 524111
Fax: (0) 1202 513293

University of Bradford
Richmond Road
Bradford
West Yorkshire BD7 1DP
Telephone: (0) 1274 733466
Fax: (0) 1274 385810
E-mail: ug-admissions@
bradford.ac.uk.
pg-admissions@bradford.ac.uk.

University of Brighton
Mithras House
Lewes Road
Brighton BN2 4AT
Telephone: (0) 1273 600900
Fax: (0) 1273 642825

University of Bristol
Senate House
Tyndall Avenue
Bristol BS8 1TH
Telephone: (0) 117-9303030
Fax: (0) 117-9251424

**University of the West of
England, Bristol**
Frenchay Campus
Coldharbour Lane
Bristol BS16 1QY
Telephone: (0) 117-965 6261
Fax: (0) 117-976 3804
E-mail: @uwe.ac.uk

Brunel University
Uxbridge
Middlesex UB8 3PH
Telephone: (0) 1895 274000
Fax: (0) 1895 232806
E-mail: @brunel.ac.uk

University of Buckingham
Hunter Street
Buckingham MK18 1EG
Telephone: (0) 1280 814080
Fax: (0) 1280 822245

University of Cambridge
University Registry
The Old Schools
Cambridge CB2 1TN
Telephone: (0) 1223 332200
Fax: (0) 1223 332332

City University
Northampton Square
London EC1V OHB
Telephone: (0) 171-477 8000
Fax: (0) 171-477 8559

Coventry University
Priory Street
Coventry CV1 5FB
Telephone: (0) 1203 631313
Fax: (0) 1203 838793
Telex: (0) 1203 838793
E-mail: dir007@coventry.ac.uk
or: ca78@cityscape.co.uk.

Cranfield University
Cranfield
Bedford MK43 OAL
Telephone: (0) 1234 750111
Fax: (0) 1234 752462
Telex: 825072 CITECHG

De Montfort University:

Leicester Campus
The Gateway
Leicester LE1 9BH
Telephone: (0) 116 2551551
Fax: (0) 116 2550307
Telex: 9312110351

Bedford Campus
37 Landsdowne Road
Bedford
MK40 2BZ
Telephone: (0) 1234 351966
Fax: (0) 1234 350833

Lincoln Campus
Caythorpe Court
Caythorpe
Grantham
Lincolnshire NG32 3EP
Telephone: (0) 1400 272521
Fax: (0) 1400 272722

Milton Keynes Campus
Kents Hill
Hammerwood Gate
Milton Keynes MK7 6HP
Telephone: (0) 1905 695511
Fax: (0) 1905 695581

University of Derby
Kedleston Road
Derby DE22 1GB
Telephone: (0) 1332 622222
Fax: (0) 1332 294861
E-mail: U.L.Ladwa@derby.ac.uk.

University of Dundee
Nethergate
Dundee DD1 4HN
Telephone: (0) 1382 223181
Fax: (0) 1382 201604
E-mail:
M.J.HENRY@dundee.ac.uk.

University of Durham
Old Shire Hall
Old Elvet
Durham DH1 3HP
Telephone: (0) 191-374 2000
Fax: (0) 191-374 3740
E-mail: j.l.hobbs@durham.ac.uk.

**University of East Anglia
International Office**
The Registry
University of East Anglia
Norwich NR4 7TJ
Telephone: (0) 1603 592048
Fax: (0) 1603 458596
E-mail: N.Perowne@uea.ac.uk.
or: Julie.Lane@uea.ac.uk.

University of East London:

Barking Campus
Longbridge Road
Dagenham
Essex RM8 2AS
Telephone: (0) 181-590 7722
Fax: (0) 181-590 7799
E-mail: G.A.ParryY@uel.ac.uk.

Stratford Campus
Romford Road
London E15 4LZ
Telephone: (0) 181-590 7722
Fax: (0) 181-519 3740

University of Edinburgh
Old College
South Bridge
Edinburgh EH8 9YL
Telephone: (0) 131-650 1000
Fax: (0) 131-650 2147
Telex: 727442 (UNIVED G)

University of Essex
Wivenhoe Park
Colchester CO4 3SQ
Telephone: (0) 1206 873333
Fax: (0) 1206 873410
E-mail: admit@essex.ac.uk.

University of Exeter
Registrar and Secretary's
Department
Northcote House
The Queen's Drive
Exeter EX4 4QJ
Telephone: (0) 1392 263263
Fax: (0) 1392 263108
E-mail: pa lee @ exeter.ac.uk.

University of Glamorgan
Pontypridd
Mid Glamorgan CF37 1DL
Telephone: (0) 1443 480480
Fax: (0) 1443 480558

University of Glasgow
Glasgow G12 8QQ
Telephone: (0) 141-339 8855
Fax: (0) 141-330 5440
Telex: 777070

Glasgow Caledonian University
70 Cowcaddens Road
Glasgow G4 OBA
Telephone: (0) 141-331 3000
Fax: (0) 141-331 3005

University of Greenwich
Wellington Street
Woolwich
London SE18 6PF
Telephone: (0) 181-331 8000
Fax: (0) 181-331 8145
E-mail: H.J.Fowler@ Greenwich.
ac.uk.

Heriot-Watt University
Riccarton
Edinburgh EH14 4AS
Telephone: (0) 131-449 5111
Fax: (0) 131-449 5153
E-mail: P.S.Mclean@ admin. hw.
ac.uk.

University of Hertfordshire
Hatfield Campus
College Lane
Hatfield
Hertfordshire AL10 9AB
Telephone: (0) 1707 284000
Fax: (0) 1707 284115
Telex: 262413

University of Huddersfield
Queensgate
Huddersfield HD1 3DH
Telephone: (0) 1484 422288
Fax: (0) 1484 516151

University of Hull
Cottingham Road
Hull HU6 7RX
Telephone: (0) 1482 346311
Fax: (0) 1482 469536
E-mail: K.F.Colquhoun@
admin.hull.ac.uk.

University of Humberside
Cottingham Road
Hull HU6 7RT
Telephone: (0) 1482 440550
Fax: (0) 1482 471343

Keele University
Keele
Staffordshire ST5 5BG
Telephone: (0) 1782 621111
Fax: (0) 1782 613847
E-mail: aaa06@admin.keele.ac.uk.

**University of Kent at
Canterbury**
Canterbury
Kent CT2 7NZ
Telephone: (0) 1227 764000
Fax: (0) 1227 452196

Kingston University
Penrhyn Road
Kingston upon Thames
Surrey KT1 1LQ
Telephone: (0) 181-547 2000
Fax: (0) 181-547 7093

**University of Central
Lancashire**
Corporation Street
Preston PR1 2HE
Telephone: (0) 1772 201201
Fax: (0) 1772 892946

Lancaster University
Bailrigg
Lancaster LA1 4YW
Telephone: (0) 1524 65201
Fax: (0) 1524 846243
E-mail: J.Gillison@lancaster.
ac.uk.

University of Leeds
Woodhouse Lane
Leeds LS2 9JT
Telephone: (0) 113 2431751
Fax: (0) 113 233 3991

Leeds Metropolitan University
Calverley Street
Leeds LS1 3HE
Telephone: (0) 113 283 2600
(*switchboard)*
(0) 113 283 3113/4 (*course enquiries)*
(0) 113 283 3115 (*general)*
E-mail: Course-Enquiries@LMU.
ac.uk.

University of Leicester
University Road
Leicester LE1 7RH
Telephone: (0) 116 252 2522
Fax: (0) 116 252 2447
Telex: 347250 LEICUN G
E-mail: @Leicester.ac.uk.

University of Liverpool
Abercromby Square
PO Box 147
Liverpool L69 3BX
Telephone: (0) 151-794 2000
Fax: (0) 151-708 6502
Telex: 627095 UNILPL G

Liverpool John Moores University
Rodney House
70 Mount Pleasant
Liverpool L3 5UX
Telephone: (0) 151-231 3584
Fax: (0) 151-707 0936

University of London
Senate House
Malet Street
London WC1E 7HU
Telephone: (0) 171-636 8000
Fax: (0) 171-636 5875
Telex: 269500 SH UL

Institutions affiliated to the University of London

Birkbeck College
Malet Street
London WC1E 7HX
Telephone: (0) 171-580 6622
Fax: (0) 171-631 6270
E-mail: c.bray@admin.
bbk.ac.uk.

British Postgraduate Medical Federation
33 Millman Street
London WC1N 3EJ
Telephone: (0) 171-831 6222
Fax: (0) 171-831 1387

Members:
Institute of Cancer Research
Institute of Child Health
Institute of Dental Surgery
The Hunterian Institute
National Heart and Lung
Institute
Institute of Neurology
Institute of Opthalmology
Institute of Psychiatry

Charing Cross and Westminster Medical School
The Reynolds Building
St Dunstan's Road
Hammersmith
London W6 8RP
Telephone: (0) 181-846 7202
Fax: (0) 181-846 7222

Courtauld Institute of Art
Somerset House
Strand
London WC2R ORN
Telephone: (0) 171-873 2414
Fax: (0) 171-873 2410
E-mail: R.Walker@CIA.lou.ac.uk

Goldsmiths' College
Lewisham Way
London SE14 6NW
Telephone: (0) 171-919 7171
Fax: (0) 171-919 7517

Heythrop College
(Theology and philosophy
are the only courses
studied at this college)
Kensington Square
London W8 5HQ
Telephone: (0) 171-795 6600
Fax: (0) 171-795 4200

Imperial College of Science, Technology and Medicine
London SW7 2AZ
Telephone: (0) 171-589 5111
Fax: (0) 171-594 8004
E-mail: L.Richardson @ ic.ac.uk

Institute of Commonwealth Studies
28 Russell Square
London WC1B 5DS
Telephone: (0) 171-580 5876
Fax: (0) 171-255 2160
E-mail: r.kochanowska@sas.ac.uk.

Institute of Education
20 Bedford Way
London WC1H OAL
Telephone: (0) 171-580 1122
Fax: (0) 171-612 6126

Institute of Germanic Studies
29 Russell Square
London WC1B 5DP
Telephone: (0) 171-580 2711
Fax: (0) 171-436 3497

Institute of Latin American Studies
31 Tavistock Square
London WC1H 9HA
Telephone: (0) 171-387 5671
Fax: (0) 171-388 5024
E-mail: ilas@sas.ac.uk

King's College London
Strand
London WC2R 2LS
Telephone: (0) 171-836 5454
Fax: (0) 171-836 1799

King's College School of Medicine and Dentistry
Bessemer Road
London SE5 9PJ
Telephone: (0) 171-737 4000
Exts. 4017 (*Medicine*);
2528 (*Dentistry*)
Fax: (0) 171-346 3693

London Business School
Sussex Place
Regent's Park
London NW1 4SA
Telephone: (0) 171-262 5050
Fax: (0) 171-724 7875
E-mail: mba-info @lbs.lon.ac.uk

The **London Hospital Medical College** has merged with **Queen Mary and Westfield College**.

London School of Economics and Political Science
Houghton Street
London WC2A 2AE
Telephone: (0) 171-405 7686
Fax: (0) 171- 831 1684
Telex: 24655 LSELON G

London School of Hygiene and Tropical Medicine
Keppel Street
London WC1E 7HT
Telephone: (0) 171-927 2239
Fax: (0) 171-323 0638
Telex: 8953474

Queen Mary and Westfield College
Mile End Road
London E1 4NS
Telephone: (0) 171-975 5555
Fax: (0) 171-975 5500

Royal Academy of Music
Marylebone Road
London NW1 5HT
Telephone: (0) 171-935 5461
Fax: (0) 171-873 7374

Royal College of Music
Prince Consort Road
London SW7 2BS
Telephone: (0) 171-589 3643
Fax: (0) 171-589 7740

Royal Free Hospital School of Medicine
Rowland Hill Street
London NW3 2PF
Telephone: (0) 171-794 0500
Ext: 4257/4258
Fax: (0) 171-794 3505

Royal Holloway
Egham Hill
Egham
Surrey TW20 OEX
Telephone: (0) 1784 434455
Fax: (0) 1784 437520

Royal Postgraduate Medical School
School Registry
Hammersmith Hospital
Du Cane Road
London W12 ONN
Telephone: (0) 181-740 3118
Fax: (0) 181-743 6764

Royal Veterinary College
Royal College Street
London NW1 OTU
Telephone: (0) 171-468 5000
Fax: (0) 171-338 2342

St Bartholomew's Hospital Medical College
West Smithfield
London EC1A 7BE
Telephone: (0) 171-982 6000
Fax: (0) 171-796 3753

St George's Hospital Medical School
Cranmer Terrace
Tooting
London SW17 ORE
Telephone: (0) 181-672 9944
Fax: (0) 181-725 3426

St Mary's Hospital Medical School
Norfolk Place
London W2 1PG
Telephone: (0) 171- 723 1252
Fax: (0) 171-724 7349

School of Oriental and African Studies
Thornhaugh Street
Russell Square
London WC1H OXG
Telephone: (0) 171-637 2388
Fax: (0) 171-436 4211
E-mail: Registrar@soas.ac.uk.

School of Pharmacy
29–39 Brunswick Square
London WC1N 1AX
Telephone: (0) 171-753 5831
Fax: (0) 171-753 5829

School of Slavonic and East European Studies
Senate House, Malet Street
London WC1E 7HU
Telephone: (0) 171-637 4934
Fax: (0) 171-436 8916
E-mail: cmorley@ssees.ac.uk

Trinity College of Music
11–13 Mandeville Place
London W1M 6AQ
Telephone: (0) 171-935 5773
Fax: (0) 171-224 6278

UMDS – Guy's and St Thomas's Medical School
Lambeth Palace Road
London SE1 7EH
Telephone: (0) 171-922 8013
Fax: (0) 171-928 0069

University College London
Gower Street
London WC1E 6BT
Telephone: (0) 171-387 7050
Fax: (0) 171-387 8057

Wye College
Wye, Ashford
Kent TN25 5AH
Telephone: (0) 1233 812401
Fax: (0) 1233 813320
Telex: 94017832 WYEC G
E-mail: academic.registrar @wye. ac.uk.

The following **University of London** institutions can be contacted through the University of London *(see above for addresses and telephone numbers)*

British Institute in Paris
Institute of Advanced Legal Studies
Institute of Classical Studies
Institute of Historical Research
Institute of United States Studies
Jews' College
Institute of Romance Studies
Warburg Institute

London Guildhall University
113 Whitechapel
High Street
London E1 7QA
Telephone: (0) 171-320 1000
Fax: (0) 171-320 3462

Loughborough University of Technology
Ashby Road, Loughborough
Leicestershire LE11 3TU
Telephone: (0) 1509 263171, ext. 4009
Fax: (0) 1509 265687
Telex: 34319

University of Luton
Park Square
Luton LU1 3JU
Telephone: (0) 1582 34111
Fax: (0) 1582 489323

University of Manchester
Oxford Road
Manchester M13 9PL
Telephone: (0) 161-275 2000
Fax: (0) 161-275 2407

Manchester Business School
Booth Street West
Manchester M15 6PB
Telephone: (0) 161-275 6311
Fax: (0) 161-275 6489
E-mail: h.e.ward@fs2.mbs.ac.uk.

University of Manchester Institute of Science and Technology
PO Box 88
Sackville Street
Manchester M60 1QD
Telephone: (0) 161-236 3311
Fax: (0) 161-228 7040
E-mail: intoff@umist.ac.uk
Telex: 666094 UMIST G

Manchester Metropolitan University
All Saints
Manchester M15 6BH
Telephone: (0) 161-247 2000
Fax: (0) 161-247 6390

Middlesex University
White Hart Lane
Tottenham
London N17 8HR
Telephone: (0) 181-362 5000
Fax: (0) 181-362 6878

Napier University
219 Colinton Road
Edinburgh EH14 1DJ
Telephone: (0) 131-444 2266
Fax: (0) 131-455 7209

University of Newcastle upon Tyne
Admissions Office
6–10 Kensington Terrace
Newcastle upon Tyne NE1 7RU
Telephone: (0) 191-222 8672/6107
Fax: (0) 191-222 6139
E-mail: Julia.Cooper@ncl.ac.uk
or: Ken Young @ncl.ac.uk
Telex: 53654 (UNINEW G)

University of North London
166–220 Holloway Road
London N7 8DB
Telephone: (0) 171-607 2789
Fax: (0) 171-753 5166
E-mail: unl.ac.uk

University of Northumbria at Newcastle
Ellison Place
Newcastle upon Tyne NE1 8ST
Telephone: (0) 191-232 6002
Fax: (0) 191-227 4017

University of Nottingham
International Office
University Park
Nottingham NG7 2 RD
Telephone: (0) 1159 9515151
Fax: (0) 115 9513666
E-mail: international.office@
nottingham.ac.uk

Nottingham Trent University
Burton Street
Nottingham NG1 4BU
Telephone: (0) 115 9418418
Fax: (0) 115 9486530

The Open University
PO Box 200
Walton Hall
Milton Keynes MK7 6YZ
Telephone: (0) 1908 653231
Fax: (0) 1908 653744

University of Oxford
University Offices
Wellington Square
Oxford OX1 2JD
Telephone: (0) 1865 270207
Fax: (0) 1865 270708
E-mail: admindpt@vax.ox.ac.uk

Oxford Brookes University
Gipsy Lane
Headington
Oxford OX3 0BP
Telephone: (0) 1865 483039
Fax: (0) 1865 483983
E-mail: prosp@brookes.ac.uk
Telex: 8314 VIA OR G

University of Paisley:

High Street
Paisley
Renfrewshire PA1 2BE
Telephone: (0) 141-848 3859
Fax: (0) 141-848 3682

(Craige Campus in Ayr Faculty of Education)
Beech Grove
Ayr KA8 0SR
Telephone: (0) 1292 4260321
Fax: (0) 1292 611705
E-mail: LIV-CSO@paisley.ac.uk

University of Plymouth
Drake Circus, Plymouth
Devon PL4 8AA
Telephone: (0) 1752 232158
Fax: (0) 1752 232141

University of Portsmouth
University House
Winston Churchill Avenue
Portsmouth PO1 2UP
Telephone: (0) 1705 876543
Fax: (0) 1705 843082

University of Reading
Whiteknights
PO Box 217
Reading RG6 6AH
Telephone: (0) 1734 316586
Fax: (0) 1734 318924
Telex: 847813

Robert Gordon University
Schoolhill
Aberdeen AB9 1FR
Telephone: (0) 1224 262000
Fax: (0) 1224 263000

University of St Andrews
Old Union Building
St Andrews
Fife KY16 9AJ
Telephone: (0) 1334 476161
Fax: (0) 1334 462543
E-mail: mish@st-and.ac.uk

University of Salford
Salford M5 4WT
Telephone: (0) 161-745 5000
Fax: (0) 161-745 5999
Telex: 668680

University of Sheffield
Admissions Office
14 Favell Road
Sheffield S3 7QX
Telephone: (0) 114 276 8555
Fax: (0) 114 272 8014
E-mail:
A.Hindmarsh@Sheffield.ac.uk

Sheffield Hallam University
City Campus
Pond Street
Sheffield S1 1WB
Telephone: (0) 114 272 0911
(switchboard) (0) 114 253 2037
(registry)
Fax: (0) 114 2534023
Telex: 54680 SH POLY GT

South Bank University
103 Borough Road
London SE1 0AA
Telephone: (0) 171-928 8989
Fax: (0) 171-815 8155
E-mail: prendep@sbu.ac.uk

University of Southampton
Highfield
Southampton SO17 1BJ
Telephone: (0) 1703 595000
Fax: (0) 1703 593037

Staffordshire University
College Road
Stoke-on-Trent ST4 2DE
Telephone: (0) 1782 294000
Fax: (0) 1782 745422

University of Stirling
Stirling FK9 4LA
Telephone: (0) 1786 473171
Fax: (0) 1786 466800
E-mail: jcmm/@STIRL.ac.uk

University of Strathclyde
McCance Building
16 Richmond Street
Glasgow G1 1XQ
Telephone: (0) 141-552 4400
Fax: (0) 141-552 5860
Telex: UNSLIB-G

University of Sunderland
Langham Tower
Ryhope Road
Sunderland SR2 7EE
Telephone: (0) 191-515 3000
Fax: (0) 191-510 2203

University of Surrey
Guildford
Surrey GU2 5XH
Telephone: (0) 1483 300800
Fax: (0) 1483 300803
E-mail: eds 1 fh@surrey.ac.uk

University of Sussex
Falmer
Brighton BN1 9RH
Telephone: (0) 1273 606755
Fax: (0) 1273 678545

University of Teesside
Borough Road
Middlesbrough
Cleveland TS1 3BA
Telephone: (0) 1642 218121
Fax: (0) 1642 342067

Thames Valley University
St Mary's Road
Ealing
London W5 5AA
Telephone: (0) 181-579 5000
Fax: (0) 181-231 2900

University of Ulster
Cromore Road
Coleraine
Co. Londonderry BT52 1SA
Telephone: (0) 1265 44141
Fax: (0) 1265 324927
E-mail: M.Green@ulst.ac.uk.

University of Wales
Registry
King Edward VII Avenue
Cathays Park
Cardiff CF1 3NS
Telephone: (0) 1222 382656
Fax: (0) 1222 396040

St David's University College
Lampeter
Dyfed SA48 7ED
Telephone: (0) 1570 422351
Fax: (0) 1570 423423

**University College of North
Wales, Bangor**
Bangor
Gwynedd LL57 2DG
Telephone: (0) 1248 351151
(switchboard)
(0) 1248 382026 (*Admissions
Office*)
Fax: (0) 1248 370451
E-mail: [K102]@UK.AC.BANGOR

**University College of
Swansea**
Singleton Park
Swansea SA2 8PP
Telephone: (0) 1792 295132
Fax: (0) 1792 295618

**University College of Wales,
Aberystwyth**
Old College, King Street
Aberystwyth
Dyfed SY23 2AX
Telephone: (0) 1970 692020
Fax: (0) 1970 622239

**University of Wales College of
Cardiff**
Postgraduate Registry
PO Box 495
Cardiff CF1 3 XD
Telephone: (0) 1222-874413
(Postgraduate Registry)
(0) 1222-874000 (switchboard)
Fax: (0) 1222-874130 (Registry)
E-mail: CARDIFF.AK.UK

**University of Wales College of
Medicine**
Heath Park
Cardiff CF4 4XN
Telephone: (0) 1222-747747
Fax: (0) 1222-742914

University of Warwick
Gibbet Hill Road
Coventry CV4 7AL
Telephone: (0) 1203 523523
Fax: (0) 1203 524442
Telex: 317472 UNIREG

University of Westminster
309 Regent Street
London W1R 8AL
Telephone: (0) 171-911 5000
(0) 171-911 5103 (*Rectorate*)
Fax: (0) 171-911 5118
(*course enquiries*)

University of Wolverhampton
Academic Planning and
Systems Unit
23 Lichfield Street
Wolverhampton
Telephone: (0) 1902 321000
Fax: (0) 1902 322680
E-mail: 1N4145 @W/V.ac.uk

University of York
Heslington
York YO1 5DD
Telephone: (0) 1904 430000
Fax: (0) 1904 433538

Colleges and institutes of higher education

**Anglo-European College
of Chiropractic**
13-15 Parkwood Road
Boscombe
Bournemouth BH5 2DF
Telephone: (0) 1202 436200
Fax: (0) 1202 436312

Bangor Normal College
George Site, Holyhead Road
Bangor, Gwynedd LL57 2PX
Telephone: (0) 1248 370171
Fax: (0) 1248 370461

Bath College of Higher Education
Newton Park
Bath BA2 9BN
Telephone: (0) 1225 873701
Fax: (0) 1225 874123

Bedford College of Higher Education
37 Lansdowne Road
Bedford MK40 2BZ
Telephone: (0) 1234 351966
Fax: (0) 1234 350833

Bishop Grosseteste College
Lincoln LN1 3DY
Telephone: (0) 1522 527347
Fax: (0) 1522 530243

Bolton Institute of Higher Education
Deane Road
Bolton
Lancashire BL3 5AB
Telephone: (0) 1204 528851
Fax: (0) 1204 399074

Bretton Hall College
Bretton Hall
West Bretton
Wakefield
West Yorkshire WF4 4LG
Telephone: (0) 1924 830261
Fax: (0) 1924 832016

**Buckinghamshire College
(a college of Brunel University)**
Queen Alexandra Road
High Wycombe
Buckinghamshire HP11 2JZ
Telephone: (0) 1494 522141
Fax: (0) 1494 524392
E-mail: cstagg01@uk.ac.
buckscol

Camberwell College of Arts School of Applied and Graphic Arts
Peckham Road
Peckham
London SE5 8UF
Telephone: (0) 171-703 0987
Fax: (0) 171-252 7347

Camborne School of Mines
Pool, Redruth
Cornwall TR15 3SE
Telephone: (0) 1209 714866
Fax: (0) 1209 716977

Canterbury Christ Church College
North Holmes Road
Canterbury
Kent CT1 1QU
Telephone: (0) 1227 767700
Fax: (0) 1227 781558

Cardiff Institute of Higher Education
PO Box 377
Llandaff Centre
Western Avenue
Cardiff CF5 2SG
Telephone: (0) 1222 551111
Fax: (0) 1222 506911
E-mail: POSTERMASTER@ cihe
ac.uk

Central School of Speech and Drama
Embassy Theatre
Eton Avenue
London NW3 3HY
Telephone: (0) 171-586 3512
Fax: (0) 171-722 4132

**Charlotte Mason College
(a college of Lancaster University)**
Rydal Road
Ambleside
Cumbria LA22 0BL
Telephone: (0) 15394 33066
Fax: (0) 15394 30305

Cheltenham and Gloucester College of Higher Education
PO Box 220
The Park Campus
Cheltenham
Gloucestershire GL50 2QF
Telephone: (0) 1242 532700
Fax: (0) 1242 532810
E-mail:POSTMASTER@
CHELT.AC.UK

Chester College of Higher Education
Cheyney Road
Chester CH1 4BJ
Telephone: (0) 1244 375444
Fax: (0) 1244 373379

Chichester Institute of Higher Education
The Dome
Upper Bognor Road
Bognor Regis
West Sussex PO21 1HR
Telephone: (0) 1243 865581
Fax: (0) 1243 828351

The College of Guidance Studies
College Road
Hextable
Kent BR8 7RN
Telephone: (0) 1322 664407
Fax: (0) 1322 613265
E-mail: ENQUIRIES@cogs.ac.uk.

Cumbria College of Art and Design
Brampton Road
Carlisle CA3 9AY
Telephone: (0) 1228 25333
Fax: (0) 1228 514491

Dartington College of Arts
Higher Close
Totnes
Devon TQ9 6EJ
Telephone: (0) 1803 862224
Fax: (0) 1803 863569
E-mail: library@dcolarts. demon. co.uk (library only)

Duncan of Jordanstone College (a faculty of the University of Dundee)
Perth Road
Dundee DD1 4HT
Telephone: (0) 1382 223261
Fax: (0) 1382 227304

Edge Hill College of Higher Education
St Helen's Road
Ormskirk
Lancashire L39 4QP
Telephone: (0) 1695 575171
Fax: (0) 1695 579997
E-mail: USERID@EHCHE. AC. UK.
or:RSTAFF@ADMIN.ENCHE.AC.UK

Edinburgh College of Art
Lauriston Place
Edinburgh EH3 9DF
Telephone: (0) 131-221 6000
Fax: (0) 131-221 6001

Falmouth College of Arts
Woodlane
Falmouth
Cornwall TR11 4RA
Telephone: (0) 1326 211077
Fax: (0) 1326 211205
E-mail: Adrian Bregazzi
admin@falmouth.ac.uk

Glasgow School of Art
167 Renfrew Street
Glasgow G3 6RQ
Telephone: (0) 141-353 4514/4515/ 4517/4570
Fax: (0) 141-353 4528

Gwent College of Higher Education
Caerleon Campus
PO Box 101
Newport
Gwent NP6 1YH
Telephone: (0) 1633 430088
Fax: (0) 1633 432006

Harper Adams Agricultural College
Edgmond, Newport
Shropshire TF10 8NB
Telephone: (0) 1952 815000
Fax: (0) 1952 814783
E-mail: registrar@haac.ac.uk

Homerton College Cambridge
Hills Road
Cambridge CB2 2PH
Telephone: (0) 1223 411141

Jordanhill College (a college of the University of Strathclyde)
Jordanhill Campus
76 Southbrae Drive
Glasgow G13 1PP
Telephone: (0) 141-950 3000
Fax: (0) 141-950 3268
E-mail: j nolan @ mis stras.ac.uk

Kent Institute of Art and Design:

New Dover Road
Canterbury
Kent CT1 3AN
Telephone: (0) 1227 769371
Fax: (0) 1227 451320

Oakwood Park site
Maidstone
Kent ME16 8AG
Telephone: (0) 1622 757286
Fax: (0) 1622 692003

Fort Pitt site
Rochester
Kent ME1 1DZ
Telephone: (0) 1634 830022
Fax: (0) 1634 829461

King Alfred's College of Higher Education
Sparkford Road
Winchester
Hampshire S022 4NR
Telephone: (0) 1962 841515
Fax: (0) 1962 842280

La Sainte Union College of Higher Education
The Avenue
Southampton S017 1 BG
Telephone: (0) 1703 228761
Fax: (0) 1703 230944

Liverpool Institute of Higher Education
PO Box 6, Stand Park Road
Liverpool L16 9JD
Telephone: (0) 151-737 3000
Fax: (0) 151-737 3100

The London Institute
The London Institute Higher Education Corporation
65 Davies Street
London W1Y 2DA
Telephone: (0) 171-514 6000
Fax: (0) 171-514 6175

The following are colleges of the London Institute:

Camberwell College of Arts
Peckham Road
Camberwell
London SE5
Telephone: (0) 171-703 0987

Central St Martin's College of Art and Design
Southampton Row
London WC1 4AP
Telephone: (0) 171-753 9090, ext. 293

Chelsea College of Art and Design
Manresa Road
SW3 6LS
Telephone: (0) 171-351 3844
Fax: (0) 171-352 8721

London College of Fashion
20 John Princes Street
London W1M 0BJ
Telephone: (0) 171-514 7400
Fax: (0) 171-514 7484

London College of Printing and Distributive Trades
Elephant and Castle
London SE1 6SB
Telephone: (0) 171-514 6500,
ext. 6538
Fax: (0) 171-514 6535

Nene College
Park Campus
Moulton Park
Northampton NN2 7AL
Telephone: (0) 1604 735500
Fax: (0) 1604 720636/ 792151

Newman College
Genners Lane
Bartley Green
Birmingham B32 3NT
Telephone: (0) 121-476 1181
Fax: (0) 121-476 1196

North Devon College
Old Sticklepath Hill
Barnstaple
Devon EX31 2BQ
Telephone: (0) 1271 45291
Fax: (0) 1271 388121

The North East Wales Institute of Higher Education
Plas Coch
Mold Road
Wrexham
Clwyd LL11 2AW
Telephone: (0) 1978 290666
Fax: (0) 1978 290008

Northern College of Education (Aberdeen Campus)
Hilton Place
Aberdeen AB9 1FA
Telephone: (0) 1224 283500
Fax: (0) 1224 487046

Norwich City College
Ipswich Road
Norwich NR2 2LJ
Telephone: (0) 1603 660011
Fax: (0) 1603 760326

Norwich School of Art and Design
St George Street
Norwich NR3 1BB
Telephone: (0) 1603 610561
Fax: (0) 1601 615728

Queen Margaret College
Clerwood Terrace
Edinburgh EH12 8TS
Telephone: (0) 131-317 3000
Fax: (0) 131-317 3256
E-mail: ET DUNC@ MAIN.
QMCED.AC.UK

Ravensbourne College of Design and Communication
Walden Road
Chislehurst
Kent BR7 5SN
Telephone: (0) 181-468 7071
Fax: (0) 181-295 0728

The College of Ripon and York St John
Lord Mayor's Walk
York YO3 7EX
Telephone: (0) 1904 656771
Fax: (0) 1904 612512
E-mail: J.LINDLEY@UCRYSJ
ac.uk

Roehampton Institute
Roehampton Lane
London SW15 5PU
Telephone: (0) 181-392 3000
Fax: (0) 181-392 3131
E-mail: MAX ROEHAMPTON.
AC.UK

Rose Bruford College
Lamorbey Park
Burnt Oak Lane
Sidcup
Kent DA15 9DF
Telephone: (0) 181-300 3024
Fax: (0) 181-308 0542

Royal Scottish Academy of Music and Drama
100 Renfrew Street
Glasgow G2 3DB
Telephone: (0) 141-332 4101
Fax: (0) 141-332 8901

St Andrew's College
Duntocher Road
Bearsden
Glasgow G61 4QA
Telephone: (0) 141-943 1424
Fax: (0) 141-943 0106

College of St Mark and St John
Derriford Road
Plymouth PL6 8BH
Telephone: (0) 1752 777188
Fax: (0) 1752 761120

St Martin's College
Lancaster LA1 3JD
Telephone: (0) 1524 63446
Fax: (0) 1524 68943

St Mary's College
Belfast
191 Falls Road
Belfast BT12 6FE
Telephone: (0) 1232 327678
Fax: (0) 1232 333719

St Mary's University College
Waldergrave Road
Strawberry Hill
Twickenham
Middlesex TW1 4SX
Telephone: (0) 181-892 0051
Fax: (0) 181-744 2080

University College Salford
Frederick Road
Salford M6 6PU
Telephone: (0) 161- 736 6541
Fax: (0) 161- 745 8386

The Scottish Agricultural College
Auchincruive
Ayr KA6 5HW
Telephone: (0) 1292 520331
Fax: (0) 1292 520287

Scottish College of Textiles
Netherdale, Galashiels
Selkirkshire TD1 3HF
Telephone: (0) 1896 753351
Fax: (0) 1896 758965

Southampton Institute of Higher Education
East Park Terrace
Southampton S014 0YN
Telephone: (0) 1703 319000
Fax: (0) 1703 222259

South Devon College
Newton Road
Torquay TQ2 5BY
Telephone: (0) 1803 291212
Fax: (0) 1803 381212

Stranmillis College
Stranmillis Road
Belfast BT9 5DY
Telephone: (0) 1232 381271
Fax: (0) 1232 664423

The Surrey Institute of Art and Design
Falkner Road, Farnham
Surrey GU9 7DS
Telephone: (0) 1252 732232
Fax: (0) 1252 718313

Swansea Institute of Higher Education (formerly West Glamorgan Institute)
Townhill Road
Swansea SA2 0UT
Telephone: (0) 1792 481000
Fax: (0) 1792 208683
E-mail: LKELLEHER@ MP.SIHE. AC.UK
Telex: 48435 WGIHE

Trinity and All Saints' College
Brownberrie Lane
Horsforth
Leeds LS18 5HD
Telephone: (0) 113 283 7100
Fax: (0) 113 283 7200

Trinity College Carmarthen
Trinity College
College Road
Carmarthen
Dyfed SA31 3EP
Telephone: (0) 1267 237971
Fax: (0) 1267 230933

Trinity College of Music
11–13 Mandeville Place
London W1M 6AQ
Telephone: (0) 171-935 5773
Fax: (0) 171-224 6278

University College Scarborough
(The North Riding College)
Filey Road
Scarborough
North Yorkshire YO11 3AZ
Telephone: (0) 1723 362392
Fax: (0) 1723 370815
E-mail: gaf@uc.scarb.ac.uk

University College Warrington
(former North Cheshire
College)
Padgate Campus
Crab Lane
Warrington
Cheshire WA2 0DB
Telephone: (0) 1925 814343
Fax: (0) 1925 816077

Westhill College
Weoley Park Road
Selly Oak
Birmingham B29 6LL
Telephone: (0) 121-472 7245
Fax: (0) 121-415 5399

West London Institute
(a college of Brunel University)
Gordon House
300 St Margaret's Road
Twickenham TW1 1PT
Telephone: (0) 181- 891 0121
Fax: (0) 181 -891 0487

Westminster College
Oxford OX2 9AT
Telephone: (0) 1865 247644
Fax: (0) 1865 251847

Winchester School of Art
Park Avenue
Winchester
Hampshire S023 8DL
Telephone: (0) 1962 842500
Fax: (0) 1962 842496

Worcester College of Higher
Education
Henwick Grove
Worcester WR2 6AJ
Telephone: (0) 1905 748080
Fax: (0) 1905 748162

Writtle College
Lordship Road
Chelmsford
Essex CM1 3RR
Telephone: (0) 1245 420705
Fax: (0) 1245 420456

Appendix 4

British Council addresses

UK offices

England

Headquarters
10 Spring Gardens
London SW1A 2BN
Telephone: (0) 171-930 8466
Telex 8952201 BRICON G
Fax: (0) 171-839 6347

Medlock Street
Manchester M15 4AA
Telephone: (0) 161-957 7000
Fax: (0) 161-957 7111

11 Portland Place
London W1N 4EJ
Telephone: (0) 171-930 8466
Fax: (0) 171-389 3199

Northern Ireland

Belfast
Director Peter Lyner OBE
1 Chlorine Gardens
Belfast BT9 5DJ
Telephone: (0) 1232 666706/
666770/683880
Fax: (0) 1232 665242

Central Bureau Representative
Paul Burrows
Telephone: (0) 1232 664418

Scotland

Edinburgh
Director Tom Craig-Cameron
3 Bruntsfield Crescent
Edinburgh EH10 4HD
Telephone: (0) 131-4474716
Fax: (0) 131-452 8487

Central Bureau Secretary
Joe Wake
Telephone: (0) 131-4478024

Wales

Cardiff
Director David Higgs
28 Park Place
Cardiff CF1 3QE
Telephone: (0) 1222 397346/7/8/9
Fax: (0) 1222 237494

Offices in the UK can receive e-mail addressed as follows:
firstname.lastname@britcoun.org

Details are correct as at 9 February 1996.

A complete list of overseas offices is available from the British Council's UK Information Centres in London and Manchester.

Acronyms

AA	Automobile Association
ADAR	Art and Design Admissions Registry
ARELS	Association of Recognized English Language Services
BAC	British Accreditation Council for Independent Further and Higher Education
BASCELT	British Association of State Colleges in English Language Teaching
BPAS	British Pregnancy Advisory Service
BSI	British Standards Institute
BST	British Summer Time
BT	Britizsh Telecom
BTEC	Business and Technology Education Council
CATCH	Centralised Application to Nurse Training Clearing House
CCETSW	Central Council for Education and Training in Social Work
EEA	European Economic Area
EU	European Union
FE	Further Education
FHSA	Family Health Services Agency
GCSE	General Certificate of Secondary Education
GMT	Greenwich Mean Time
GNVQ	General National Vocational Qualification
GTTR	Graduate Teacher Training Registry
HE	Higher Education
HND	Higher National
HND	Higher National Diploma
HOST	Hosting for Overseas Students
IB	International Baccalaureate
IELTS	International English Language Testing Service
IND	Immigration and Nationality Department
LCCI	London Chamber of Commerce and Industry
MOT	Ministry of Transport
NACPME	National Advice Centre for Postgraduate Medical Education
NARIC	National Academic Recognition Information Centre
NCVQ	National Council for Vocational Qualifications
NHS	National Health Service
NI	National Insurance
NMCCH	Nurses and Midwives Central Clearing House
NUS	National Union of Students
ODASS	Overseas Development Administration Shared Scholarships
ORSAS	Overseas Research Student Awards Scheme

PEOs	Public Enquiry Offices	TOEFL	Test of English as a Foreign Language
PGCE	Postgraduate Certificate of Education	UCAS	Universities and Colleges Admissions System
RAC	Royal Automobile Club		
RADAR	Royal Association for Disability and Rehabilitation	UCLES	University of Cambridge Local Examinations Syndicate
RSA	Royal Society of Arts		
SCE	Scottish Certificate of Education	UK	United Kingdom
SCOTVEC	Scottish Vocational Education Council	UKCOSA	UK Council for International Education
SKILL	National Bureau for Students with Disabilities	VAT	value added tax
		YHA	Youth Hostels Association
SVQ	Scottish Vocational Qualification	YMCA	Young Men's Christian Association
SWAS	Social Work Admissions System	YWCA	Young Women's Christian Association
TEFL	Teaching English as a Foreign Language		

Index